Monetized

From Content Creator to Revenue Generator

Michael Piepkorn

Copyright © 2024 Michael Piepkorn

All rights reserved.

ISBN: 9798327056091

Imprint: Independently published

DEDICATION

To the hardworking entrepreneurs, content creators, and relentless hustlers who dare to dream big and grind daily. This book is for you—the visionaries who turn passion into profit, the innovators who transform ideas into income, and the relentless spirits who never give up. Your dedication, creativity, and unwavering determination inspire us all. May this book help you unlock new paths to success and take your journey to the next level. Keep pushing, keep creating, and keep monetizing.

TABLE OF CONTENTS

Understanding Value 7

    Platform 21

    Affiliate Marketing 24

    Merchandising / Branded Apparel 28

    Backup YouTube Channel 31

    Physical Content Sales 34

    Sponsorships and Advertisements 39

    Community Donation Platforms 45

    Supercuts and Reusing Content 50

    Expand Social Media Presence 54

    Podcasting 58

    Add Languages 61

Educational and Informational Content 65

    Online Courses 67

    Writing and Publishing a Book 70

    Public Speaking Engagements 74

    Consulting Services 78

    Webinars 82

Creative and Artistic Channels 85

    Photography and Art 87

Monetized

- Digital Products 91
- Subscription Boxes 95
- App Development 99
- Destination Centers 103

Lifestyle content and Personal Vlogs 107

- Meet and Greets 109
- Physical Products 115
- Life Coaching 119
- Freelance Writing 123
- Events, Trips, and Tours 125

Entertainment, Media, and News Channels 129

- Interactive Live Streams / Super Chats 131
- Crowdfunding 134
- Event Coverage Contracts 139

Gaming Content Creators and Streamers 143

- Game Development 145
- Game Mod Development 149
- Game Tournaments 153
- Hosting a Gaming Server 158

ACKNOWLEDGMENTS

To my many business mentors throughout my career, your guidance, wisdom, and unwavering support have been invaluable. You have shaped my professional journey and inspired me to reach new heights. Thank you for sharing your knowledge and for believing in me.

To the numerous consultation clients who have entrusted me with their businesses, thank you for allowing me the privilege to assist and collaborate with you. Your trust and partnership have been instrumental in my growth and understanding of the entrepreneurial landscape. Each of you has taught me valuable lessons and reinforced the importance of resilience and innovation.

To the content creators who generously contributed their insights and experiences, this book would not have been possible without your valuable input. Your dedication to your craft and willingness to share your journeys have laid the foundation for these pages' strategies and advice. Thank you for your openness and for being an integral part of this project.

Together, you have all made this book a reality. Thank you for your inspiration, trust, and contribution

"Monetized" focuses on strategies for content creators to make money beyond just video royalties. The traditional ad revenue model is often not enough to support content creators full-time, and this book explores various alternative business models to help you monetize your audience and content effectively. It delves into diverse business models, including advertising, affiliate marketing, brand partnerships, and merchandise creation. These strategies are presented within the context of different content genres, ensuring that creators from various genres can find effective ways to generate income. However, these strategies are flexible and can be adapted by content creators according to their unique strengths and brand identity. It's essential to recognize that not all methods will suit every channel. The book aims to present the options and let the reader adopt them if they fit their strengths and branding.

First, let us explore some basic principles of monetizing content creation.

UNDERSTANDING VALUE

Understanding the value of your channel is crucial for effective monetization. This value comprises three key components: subscribers, content, and brand value. Each element plays a pivotal role in your overall success and income generation.

SUBSCRIBERS

Subscribers are the primary metric by which success can be measured and predicted. Building a robust subscriber base should be a primary goal, as their loyalty provides a stable foundation for all monetization strategies.

Subscribers represent your most loyal audience members who regularly engage with your content. They watch your videos, leave comments, share your posts, and participate in community discussions. Such consistent engagement boosts your visibility on content platforms since many algorithms favor content with high engagement rates. Loyal subscribers can help propel your content to a broader audience, increasing your reach and influence.

Additionally, loyal subscribers are more inclined to consume new content as soon as it is released, ensuring a steady stream of views and interactions. This immediate engagement can lead to higher rankings in search results and recommendations, further amplifying your presence on the platform.

Monetizing this loyal audience opens several lucrative opportunities, many of which will be described in this book. Most generate additional income and strengthen the bond between you and your audience.

By leveraging your subscribers and channel as a marketing outlook for other business opportunities, you can maximize your channel's potential for consistent and growing revenue.

Subscribers also enhance your credibility and trustworthiness as a content creator. Their support signals potential new viewers that your content is valuable and reliable. This trust can lead to word-of-mouth promotion, expanding your reach organically. Furthermore, a loyal subscriber base can attract collaboration opportunities with brands and other creators as these entities seek to partner with influencers with a committed audience.

Building a sense of community is another invaluable aspect of having subscribers. A strong community fosters loyalty and engagement, creating a supportive environment where subscribers feel connected to you and each other. This sense of belonging can lead to higher retention rates and a more engaged audience, further solidifying your foundation for growth and monetization.

Additionally, subscribers play a crucial role in influencing platform algorithms. Content platforms like YouTube and Twitch use algorithms to recommend videos to users. A high number of engaged subscribers can positively affect these algorithms. Subscriber interactions—such as likes, comments, and shares—signal to the algorithms that your content is valuable and engaging, boosting your content's visibility and discovery.

By leveraging these strategies, you can optimize the monetization potential of your subscriber base, leading to a stable and growing revenue stream. Consistent content creation is paramount to building a solid subscriber base. Regularly posting high-quality content builds anticipation and trust, as subscribers know they can expect new material from you on a predictable schedule. Diversifying your content to include different formats, such as tutorials, live streams, and Q&A sessions, can cater to a broader range of interests within your subscriber base, keeping them engaged and coming back for more.

Content Consistency and Diversification

Consistent content creation is critical to building a substantial and loyal subscriber base. Regularly posting high-quality content helps build anticipation and trust as subscribers come to expect new material from you on a predictable schedule. Consistency not only maintains your current audience but also attracts new viewers. Diversify your content formats to cater to a broader range of interests. Including tutorials, live streams, and Q&A sessions can engage a wider audience and keep them returning for more.

Engagement and Interaction

Engagement and interaction are critical in cultivating a loyal subscriber base. Actively engaging with your audience by responding to comments, hosting live Q&A sessions, and creating interactive content helps build stronger relationships with your subscribers. Such interaction makes subscribers feel valued and appreciated, deepening their connection to your brand. For instance, responding thoughtfully to comments fosters a sense of community and encourages more viewers to join the conversation.

Communicating Subscriber Value

Communicating the value of subscribing to your channel is crucial. Highlight the benefits subscribers will receive, such as exclusive content, community access, and special perks. Offering incentives for subscribing, such as giveaways or shout-outs, can further encourage viewers to become subscribers. Make these benefits explicit in your content and promotional materials to convert casual viewers into loyal subscribers.

Cross-Promotion and Collaboration

Cross-promotion is another effective strategy for attracting new subscribers. Promote your content across various platforms and collaborate with other creators to introduce your channel to new audiences. Guest appearances, joint projects, and cross-promotional campaigns can drive traffic to your primary channel and convert casual viewers into dedicated subscribers. For example, a joint livestream with another popular creator can exponentially increase your exposure and attract a new segment of their audience to your channel.

Monetized

Regular Analysis and Adaptation

Regular analysis and adaptation of your content strategy are crucial for sustained growth. You can monitor engagement metrics, viewer demographics, and overall content performance by utilizing analytics tools like YouTube Analytics or Twitch Insights. This data helps you identify popular content themes, optimal posting times, and demographic segments most engaged with your material. Understanding these elements allows you to tailor your content strategy to meet your audience's expectations better and attract new subscribers effectively.

CONTENT

High-quality content is the cornerstone of any successful content creation strategy. Regardless of your platform or monetization methods, your content must be engaging, valuable, and likable. The phrase "content is king" is often used in the digital world, and for good reason. High-quality content stands out in a sea of mediocrity, capturing and retaining viewers' attention.

Quality content is characterized by its ability to engage the audience, provoke thought, entertain, or provide valuable information. Whether you are producing videos, blog posts, podcasts, or any other form of media, the goal should always be to create content that resonates with your audience. Engaging content fosters a sense of community and connection, encouraging viewers to interact with your material through comments, shares, likes, and other forms of engagement.

Understanding your audience's interests and needs allows you to tailor your content to their expectations. Likable content often has a higher shareability factor, meaning viewers are likelier to share it with their network, further extending your reach and potential subscriber base.

The Importance of Evergreen Content

While quality content is essential, the type of content you produce also plays a significant role in your long-term success. Evergreen content is a critical component of a sustainable content strategy. Evergreen content refers to material that remains relevant and valuable over an extended period, continually attracting viewers and generating income. This type of content does not rely on current trends or fleeting interests; instead, it addresses timeless topics that always have an audience.

Monetized

For example, tutorials on foundational skills, comprehensive guides, and content addressing problems can continually attract new viewers over time, unlike trend-based content that may quickly lose relevance. This long-term relevance makes it an asset in your content library, contributing consistently to your visibility and reach.

Sustained Income

Because evergreen content continually attracts viewers, it generates a consistent income stream. This consistency is crucial for maintaining financial stability and growth as a content creator. Unlike trend-driven content, which may experience rapid spikes and falls in viewership, evergreen content provides a steady, reliable source of revenue.

Reduced Pressure for Constant Content Creation

While regular content updates remain important, evergreen content reduces the pressure to produce new material constantly. High-quality evergreen pieces can continue to draw traffic and revenue, allowing you to focus on creating fewer but more impactful pieces. This balance lets you invest more time and resources into crafting high-caliber content without sacrificing engagement.

Creating Evergreen Content

To create effective evergreen content, consider the following guidelines:

Identify Timeless Topics

Focus on subjects that have long-term appeal. How-to guides, tutorials, educational content, and fundamental concepts within your niche are excellent examples of evergreen topics. These areas will continually attract audiences seeking reliable information. For instance, a comprehensive tutorial on basic photography techniques will remain relevant to new photographers for years to come.

Monetized

Ensure High Quality

The content must be well-researched, accurate, and professionally presented. High-quality evergreen content is its credential in your field, attracting more viewers and building trust. For example, a meticulously researched article or video on financial planning can become a go-to resource for viewers over many years. Future clients can reference it to determine your knowledge and capability.

Optimize for Search Engines

Use search engine optimization (SEO) techniques to ensure your content is discoverable. Proper keyword usage, clear and concise titles, and meta descriptions help improve your content's visibility in search engine results, driving organic traffic to your site. For example, keywords like "beginner's guide to SEO" can help your content rank higher in search results, attracting a wider audience.

Update as Needed

While evergreen content is designed to be timeless, reviewing and updating it periodically is essential to ensure the information remains accurate and relevant. This can help maintain its value and appeal to your audience. For example, a guide on social media marketing should be updated to reflect any changes in platform algorithms or new strategies.

You can create a robust content library that supports sustained growth and income by prioritizing high-quality, evergreen content. This strategy, combined with regular performance analysis and adaptation, will help you build a loyal subscriber base and optimize your channel for long-term success.

BRAND

Brand value is a multifaceted concept that extends beyond the content you create. It encompasses your audience's emotional connection with you, crucial to their perception and loyalty. This emotional bond can significantly impact your monetization strategies, opening numerous opportunities for partnerships, sponsorships, and merchandise. Understanding and leveraging brand value is essential for any content creator aiming to build a sustainable and profitable career.

Your brand is the manifestation of how your audience perceives you and your content. It includes the feelings and emotions your name or logo evokes in your viewers. This emotional connection can manifest in various ways, such as trust, admiration, excitement, or entertainment. When people hear your name, the emotions they recall are integral to your brand's value.

For instance, if your content consistently provides value through education, inspiration, or entertainment, your audience will develop a positive emotional connection with your brand. This connection fosters loyalty and encourages your audience to support you through various monetization channels. A strong, positive brand can:

Build Trust and Credibility: When your audience trusts you, they are more likely to engage with your content, support your ventures, and purchase your products or services. Trust is built over time through consistent, high-quality content and genuine interactions. For example, a tech reviewer known for honest, thorough reviews will attract an audience that values their insights and recommendations.

Enhance Audience Loyalty: Loyal viewers are likelier to become repeat customers, participate in community activities, and advocate for your brand. This loyalty can translate into sustained engagement and recurring revenue. For instance, a cooking channel with a loyal following might see recurring views and purchases of their cookbook.

Increase Perceived Value: A strong brand can elevate the perceived value of your content and products. This perception can justify premium pricing for exclusive content, merchandise, or services. For example, an influencer with a solid personal brand might successfully sell premium-priced courses or limited-edition merchandise.

Building and Leveraging Brand Value

To effectively build and leverage brand value, consider the following strategies...

Consistent Branding: Maintain consistency in your branding across all platforms. Use the same logo, color scheme, and tone of voice to create a recognizable and cohesive brand identity. Consistency helps reinforce your brand in the minds of your audience, making it more memorable and trustworthy.

Engage with Your Audience: Regularly interact with your audience through comments, social media, and live events. Genuine engagement fosters a deeper connection and demonstrates that you value your audience's input and support. Building this rapport is essential for creating a loyal community.

Create Emotional Content: Develop content that resonates on an emotional level. Through storytelling, addressing common pain points, or sharing personal experiences, emotional content can strengthen the bond between you and your audience. For instance, a fitness influencer sharing their fitness journey can inspire and motivate their audience, creating a deeper connection.

Leverage Testimonials and Reviews: Showcase positive testimonials and reviews from your audience or clients to build social proof. Positive feedback can enhance your credibility and attract new viewers who trust the experiences of your existing audience.

Monetized

Strategic Partnerships: Collaborate with brands and creators that align with your values and audience. Strategic partnerships can enhance your brand credibility and reach, introducing your content to new, synergistic audiences.

By understanding and leveraging brand value, you can create a powerful connection with your audience, enhancing their loyalty and unlocking many monetization opportunities. Cultivating a strong, positive brand is essential for sustaining growth and achieving long-term success in content creation.

Strategic Brand Alignment

To ensure your brand remains aligned with your audience's expectations and values, consider the following strategies:

Understand Your Audience: Regularly engage with your audience to understand their preferences, interests, and values. Surveys, comments, and social media interactions can provide valuable insights into what your audience expects from your brand. For instance, a gaming content creator might discover through social media polls that their audience is particularly interested in gameplay tutorials and live streams, guiding future content planning.

Consistent Messaging: Maintain a consistent brand voice across all your content and interactions. This consistency reinforces your brand identity and builds trust with your audience. For example, a fitness influencer should consistently project health, wellness, and motivation messages across their videos, social media posts, and merchandise.

Evaluate Opportunities Carefully: Before pursuing new monetization opportunities, assess whether they align with your brand's identity and audience's expectations. Products or services that do not fit well with your brand can dilute its value. Hence, ensuring that every new venture resonates with your core message and values is crucial.

Adapt and Evolve: While consistency is important, so is adaptability. Stay attuned to changes in your audience's interests and broader market trends. Evolving your brand in a way that stays true to its core values while meeting new demands can enhance its longevity and relevance. For instance, a tech reviewer might expand their content to include new technology trends such as virtual reality, aligning the content evolution with market changes and audience interests.

Avoiding Brand Misalignment: Brand misalignment occurs when your products or services do not resonate with your core audience. This misalignment can dilute your brand value and confuse your audience, potentially leading to decreased engagement and support.

Case Study: Mr. Beast and the Chocolate Venture

A notable example of brand misalignment is Mr. Beast's venture into the chocolate market. Known for his high-energy, engaging videos and philanthropy, Mr. Beast built a brand that resonates with excitement and entertainment. However, his leap into selling chocolate did not align well with his audience's expectations. The core audience that followed Mr. Beast for his unique content did not see the connection between his brand and the chocolate product, leading to a rough start to the venture.

Conversely, a more aligned product, like a branded streaming kit, would have likely made more sense. Given Mr. Beast's strong presence in the digital and content creation space, a product that helps aspiring content creators could have resonated better with his audience. This alignment would leverage his brand's strengths and effectively meet his audience's expectations.

By strategically aligning your brand with your audience's expectations and market conditions, you can enhance brand loyalty, maintain audience trust, and open new monetization opportunities that resonate well with your core viewers. This holistic approach ensures that your brand remains relevant, credible, and financially viable in the long term.

PLATFORM DIVERSIFICATION

For new content creators, gaining initial exposure can be a daunting challenge. The digital landscape is vast and competitive, so casting a wide net rather than relying on a single platform is essential. The popularity of social media and content websites is often cyclical, with each platform appealing to different generations and demographics. Moreover, platforms can change their algorithms and policies without notice, significantly impacting your visibility and income. Technical issues like server outages or bugs can disrupt your revenue stream and viewer engagement. In this chapter, we will explore the importance and benefits of platform diversification, focusing on how it can help content creators stabilize and grow their presence and income.

The Benefits of Multicasting

Multicasting, or streaming and posting content on multiple platforms, is an effective strategy to expand reach and engage with diverse user bases. Content creators can tap into varied markets with unique demographics and interests by leveraging platforms like YouTube, Twitch, Rumble, and Kick. This approach increases overall visibility and requires minimal additional effort since the content has already been created. Modern tools like Streamlabs OBS facilitate streaming to multiple platforms simultaneously, making multicasting a practical option for content creators.

For instance, Twitch's live-streaming focus attracts a different audience than YouTube's broad video-based community. By engaging with both, you ensure that your reach is not limited to the constraints and demographics of a single platform. This wider approach maximizes your potential audience engagement and visibility.

Platform diversification offers several strategic advantages that can enhance a content creator's reach, engagement, and revenue. Firstly, enhanced revenue streams are a vital benefit. Each platform has its own set of monetization opportunities. For instance, YouTube provides avenues for earning through ad revenue, channel memberships, and Super Chats, while Twitch offers subscriptions, bits, and ads. Additionally, platforms like Patreon allow fans to support creators directly through membership tiers and exclusive content. By leveraging multiple revenue models across various platforms, creators can diversify their income streams. This diversification makes their financial situation more robust and less susceptible to fluctuations caused by changes on any platform.

Another significant advantage is increased exposure. Different platforms attract different audiences. For example, TikTok's short-form videos are popular with a younger demographic, while Facebook's video platform appeals to an older audience. By posting content on multiple platforms, creators can reach a broader range of viewers and increase their chances of being discovered by new fans. This broader exposure can lead to higher engagement rates and a more diverse follower base.

Risk mitigation is another critical benefit of platform diversification. Relying on a single platform can be risky due to potential policy changes, algorithm updates, or technical issues that could suddenly impact visibility and income. By maintaining a presence across multiple platforms, creators can mitigate these risks. If one platform experiences issues, other platforms' content and revenue streams remain unaffected, ensuring greater stability.

Furthermore, an optimized content strategy is achievable through platform diversification. Different platforms have unique strengths and content formats that resonate with their specific audiences. For instance, Instagram and TikTok are ideal for short, visually appealing content, while YouTube is better suited for longer, more in-depth videos. By understanding and leveraging these differences, creators can tailor their content strategy to maximize engagement on each platform, ensuring their content performs well across various channels.

Monetized

Finally, community building is significantly enhanced through platform diversification. Each platform offers unique tools and features for fostering community interaction. Twitch, for instance, has a dedicated community aspect through live chat interactions and subscriber perks, while YouTube offers community posts and stories. Effectively utilizing these tools across platforms allows creators to build a stronger, more engaged community. Engaging with the audience on multiple fronts creates a more cohesive and loyal fan base, contributing to long-term success.

Practical Steps for Effective Platform Diversification

Content creators need to follow a strategic approach to diversify across platforms effectively. The first step is to identify target platforms. Research and identify which platforms align best with your content and target audience. Consider the demographics, content formats, and engagement tools each platform offers to determine where your efforts will be most impactful.

Next, leverage multicasting tools. Tools like Streamlabs OBS enable creators to stream to multiple platforms simultaneously. This approach ensures a broader audience reach without requiring significant additional effort. By multicasting, creators can maximize their visibility and engage with diverse user bases more efficiently.

Tailoring content to platform strengths is another crucial step. Adapt your content to fit the strengths and preferences of each platform. For example, create short, engaging clips for TikTok and Instagram and produce longer, more detailed videos for YouTube. Understanding the best content format for each platform ensures that your content resonates with its audience and performs well.

Active engagement with your audience on each platform is essential. Engage with your audience by responding to comments, participating in live chats, and using platform-specific features to foster community interaction. Consistent and meaningful engagement helps build a loyal and active community across all platforms.

Monetized

Finally, monitor performance and adapt. Regularly analyze the performance of your content on different platforms using analytics tools. Understand what works best and adjust your strategy accordingly. This ongoing optimization will help maximize your reach and engagement, ensuring your content remains relevant and effective across all platforms.

Following these practical steps, content creators can diversify their presence across multiple platforms, enhancing their reach, engagement, and revenue potential. Platform diversification is a powerful strategy for long-term success in the dynamic digital landscape.

Monetized

Platform	Demographic (2024)	Content Focus (2024)
YouTube	Broad, especially 18-34-year-olds	Diverse video content
Twitch	Primarily 18-34-year-old males	Live gaming and creative streams
TikTok	Predominantly 16-24-year-olds	Short-form video content
Instagram	Popular among 18-34-year-olds	Photos, short videos, Stories, and Reels
Facebook	Strong among 25-54-year-olds	Mixed content and community engagement
Snapchat	Primarily 13-24-year-olds	Short-lived photos and videos, Stories
Twitter	Significant 18-49-year-old presence	Short text updates and live streaming
Reddit	Popular with 18-34-year-old progressives	User-generated content and discussions
LinkedIn	Professionals, primarily 25-49-year-olds	Networking, job posts, industry news
Pinterest	Predominantly 18-49-year-old females	Visual content on DIY, fashion, home decor
Patreon	Creators and dedicated fans, typically 18-34-year-olds	Subscription-based exclusive content
Rumble	Broad, with 25-54-year-olds	Video content focused on free speech and monetization
Kick	Younger audience, particularly 18-34-year-olds	Live gaming and interactive content

AFFILIATE MARKETING

Affiliate marketing presents a powerful and mutually beneficial opportunity for content creators, offering a practical and profitable business model that aligns seamlessly with the digital content creation landscape. This strategy is grounded in the unique relationship between content creators and their audience, leveraging the trust and influence that creators have cultivated over time.

For creators, affiliate marketing provides a direct and scalable source of income that complements their content production; unlike ad revenue, which can be unpredictable and influenced by external factors such as algorithm changes or fluctuating ad rates, affiliate marketing offers creators more significant control over their earnings. They can select products that resonate with their content and audience, creating a more personalized and relevant marketing approach.

The success of this business model heavily relies on the audience's perception and trust in the creator. Viewers are more likely to consider purchasing products recommended by a creator they follow and trust. This trust is built over time through consistent, authentic content that aligns with the interests and needs of the audience. By recommending products that genuinely benefit or interest their viewers, creators can monetize their influence without compromising their authenticity or audience relationships.

Moreover, the vast array of products available through affiliate programs means that creators across virtually all niches can find relevant products to promote. This versatility allows creators to integrate product recommendations naturally into their content, whether it's a tech gadget in a review video, a piece of workout equipment in a fitness vlog, or a novel in a book review.

Monetized

Affiliate marketing is a logical extension of the content creation process. It empowers creators to monetize their platform in an audience-centric way and aligned with their content, ensuring a sustainable and mutually beneficial business model.

Harnessing Product Recommendations

Effective affiliate marketing begins with strategic product recommendations. Content creators should integrate these recommendations seamlessly into their content, ensuring they are relevant and valuable to their audience. The key is subtlety and alignment with the channel's niche. For example, a tech reviewer might include affiliate links to the latest gadgets they're reviewing, while a beauty vlogger could link to makeup products used in their tutorial. This integration should feel natural and add value to the viewer's experience, not disrupt it.

Utilizing the Amazon Affiliate Program

The Amazon Affiliate Program is popular due to its wide range of products and user-friendly interface. Creators can leverage this platform by linking to products they use, review, or recommend in their videos. However, they should be aware of the relatively lower commission rates. The success of using Amazon lies in the volume of sales generated through the links. Creators should regularly update these links and consider creating themed lists of products that align with their video content.

Creating a Wishlist

A wish list is a direct and transparent way for creators to engage with their audience. By sharing a wish list, content creators allow supporters to contribute more personally and meaningfully to the channel. This could include items that assist in content creation or the personal interests of the creator. The wish list can be publicized subtly in the video descriptions or during community updates, allowing fans to engage directly with the creator's needs and desires.

Monetized

Partnering for Discount Codes

Collaborating with companies to offer unique discount codes is a win-win for creators and their audiences. These codes can provide viewers with a tangible benefit, such as a discount on a product, while also driving sales for the company. For creators, it fosters audience loyalty and can be an effective way to track the direct impact of their recommendations. Announcing these codes should be done in a way that aligns with the content of the video and adds value to the viewer's experience.

Diversifying Affiliate Networks

Beyond Amazon, numerous affiliate networks offer a variety of products and potentially higher commission rates. Content creators should explore these options to find networks that best align with their channel's content and audience interests. This could involve joining specialized networks that cater to specific niches or industries. By diversifying their affiliate partnerships, creators can enhance the relevance of their product recommendations and potentially increase their earnings.

Implementing Tracking and Analytics Tools

Content creators should utilize tracking and analytics tools to manage and optimize affiliate marketing efforts effectively. These tools can provide valuable insights into which products and affiliate links perform best, helping creators understand their audience's preferences and buying behaviors. This data can then be used to tailor future recommendations and strategies. Regularly reviewing and adjusting affiliate marketing tactics based on this data is crucial for maximizing the effectiveness of this monetization strategy.

Examples

1. **Tech Review Channels**: Channels like MKBHD and Unbox Therapy use affiliate marketing to monetize their reviews of gadgets. They provide Amazon affiliate links to the reviewed products, earning a commission on sales.

2. **Lifestyle Vloggers**: Creators like Zoella often share products they use in their daily lives, from makeup to home goods, with affiliate links in their video descriptions.
3. **Fitness Channels**: Fitness influencers like Athlean-X often have affiliate partnerships with supplement companies or fitness equipment manufacturers, promoting these products in their videos.

Challenges and Considerations

One of the primary challenges in affiliate marketing is maintaining audience trust. Over-promotion or recommending irrelevant products to the audience can quickly erode this trust. Content creators must maintain authenticity by promoting products they genuinely believe in and aligning with their audience's interests. Authenticity ensures the recommendations feel natural and credible, reinforcing viewers' trust in the creator.

Regulatory compliance is another critical consideration. Creators must adhere to Federal Trade Commission (FTC) guidelines by disclosing their affiliate relationships transparently. This disclosure ensures viewers know the potential financial gain creators might receive from their recommendations. Transparency in these relationships not only complies with legal requirements but also fosters trust by being honest with the audience about the nature of the recommendations.

Ensuring content relevance is essential for practical conversions. The products promoted must align with the content and the audience's interests. Irrelevant product promotions can lead to poor conversion rates and harm the creator's reputation and audience trust. By carefully selecting products that resonate with their audience, creators can enhance the effectiveness of their affiliate marketing efforts and maintain a positive relationship with their viewers.

MERCHANDISING / BRANDED APPAREL

Content creators are not just entertainers and educators but entrepreneurs and brand builders. As audiences grow and brand loyalty strengthens, creators will have a significant opportunity to diversify their revenue streams through merchandising and branded apparel.

The merchandising model makes sense for content creators as a natural extension of their brand. It offers a tangible way for fans to support and connect with their favorite creators while providing creators with a vital income source. However, success in this arena requires more than just slapping a logo on a t-shirt; it demands a deep understanding of one's audience, strategic planning, and innovative thinking.

Print-on-Demand Services

Print on Demand (POD) services have revolutionized how creators approach merchandising. These services, like Printful, Teespring, or Redbubble, offer a seamless solution to sell merchandise without needing inventory management. The primary advantage is reducing financial risk, as products are only produced when an order is placed. This model allows creators to experiment with various designs and products, adapting to audience preferences without incurring upfront costs. YouTube personalities like Sarah from Wholesale Ted and Marques Brownlee have successfully leveraged POD services, offering a diverse range of merchandise from apparel to tech accessories, showcasing the versatility and convenience of these platforms.

Monetized

Bulk Orders for Higher Profit

While POD services offer convenience and risk mitigation, bulk ordering remains attractive for higher profit margins. This approach, however, comes with the inherent risk of unsold inventory, making it crucial for creators to estimate demand accurately. Market research and pre-order campaigns are effective strategies to gauge audience interest. Bulk orders are particularly effective for limited edition merchandise, creating a sense of urgency and exclusivity among fans. PewDiePie's approach to limited edition merchandise is an exemplary case study, where he successfully harnessed his massive following to ensure the sale of bulk-ordered products.

Beyond the T-shirt

Moving beyond traditional merchandise like t-shirts can open new revenue streams for content creators. High-margin items such as stickers, pint glasses, pillows, hats, and phone cases are increasingly popular due to recent advances in print technology. Stickers, for example, are cost-effective and offer the added advantage of being used on high-value, frequently used consumer items, enhancing brand visibility. Collaborating with professional designers or employing design tools is critical to creating high-quality, relevant, and eye-catching designs that resonate with the channel's theme and audience interests. With the flexibility offered by POD services, these items can be quickly prototyped and fulfilled, offering a low-risk avenue to test new product lines. Local print shops can also be a resource, especially for smaller, high-margin items like stickers.

Engaging Viewers in the Design Process

Engaging the audience in the design process of merchandise can significantly boost engagement and sales. This strategy fosters a sense of community and gives viewers a sense of ownership and connection with the brand. Methods like social media polls, design contests, and feedback sessions allow creators to involve their audience in making key decisions regarding merchandise. This approach has been successfully implemented by creators like MrBeast, who actively involved his audience in choosing designs for

Monetized

his merchandise line. Regular updates about the design process, showcasing prototype designs, and incorporating viewer feedback into final design decisions are effective ways to maintain audience engagement and interest in the merchandise.

BACKUP YOUTUBE CHANNEL

As highlighted in the introductory chapter, diversification is not just a strategy but a necessity for sustainable growth and risk mitigation. Operating a second channel emerges as a compelling business model for several reasons, each rooted in both the creator's and the audience's evolving needs and preferences.

Firstly, content creators often have a range of interests and skills that may not align neatly with the theme of their primary channel. A second channel offers a platform to explore these diverse interests, be it personal vlogs, behind-the-scenes content, or entirely different genres. This satisfies the creator's desire to express varied facets of their creativity and caters to audience segments with broader interests.

Moreover, the audience of any successful channel is not a monolith; it's a spectrum of viewers with varying tastes and preferences. A second channel allows creators to serve these different audience segments more effectively. For instance, some subscribers might prefer more in-depth, niche content, while others might enjoy lighter, more personal insights into the creator's life. By catering to these varied preferences, creators can strengthen their connection with a varied audience base, enhancing viewer loyalty and engagement across both channels.

Another critical aspect is risk management. Big Tech Corporations have ever-changing policies, and the looming threat of copyright issues can pose significant threats to a channel's viability. A second channel acts as a contingency plan, ensuring that the creator's online presence and income stream are not entirely disrupted in the face of challenges with the main channel.

Additionally, the second channel can serve as a testing ground for new content ideas or formats, reducing the risk of alienating the main channel's audience with untested concepts. This approach allows for gradual experimentation and refinement based on viewer feedback, leading to more successful content strategies.

From a business perspective, a second channel opens up additional revenue streams. It diversifies the creator's income sources through ad sponsorships and collaborations that may not align with the primary channel's content. This diversification is crucial in an ecosystem where income from digital content can be volatile and unpredictable.

Leveraging Cross-Promotion for Dual Channel Growth

Cross-promotion art lies in effectively teasing and highlighting content across both channels. This strategy involves strategically placing snippets or previews of content from one channel into the other. For instance, a creator might end a video on their main channel with a teaser of what's coming up on their second channel, thereby intriguing viewers and encouraging them to subscribe to both. This method increases the visibility of the second channel and adds value to the main channel's content by providing viewers with additional, related content.

Creating Synergistic Collaborative Content

Another potent strategy is to create collaborative content that spans across both channels. This could involve starting a story or a discussion on one channel and continuing it on the other, encouraging audiences to flow between the two. Such an approach drives traffic and builds a narrative bridge between the channels, making the content on each seem like part of a larger, cohesive story. This interconnected content strategy helps maintain a robust, engaged viewer base across both platforms.

Consistency in Branding and Messaging

Maintaining consistent branding and messaging across both channels is crucial for effective cross-promotion. While the content themes may differ, the underlying brand ethos should remain coherent. This

Monetized

consistency helps build a unified brand identity that audiences can easily recognize and connect with, regardless of the channel they watch. It's about creating a brand experience that is seamless and unified, one that resonates with the audience's expectations and experiences from one channel to the other.

Monetized

PHYSICAL CONTENT SALES

The business model of selling stock videos as DVDs or digital downloads represents a strategic devolution for content monetization for creators. This approach is anchored in maximizing the value of existing intellectual property. Having built a substantial library of videos, content creators find in this model an opportunity to repurpose and monetize their existing assets beyond their initial online viewership. It's a method that extracts additional value from what has already been created and breathes new life into older content.

Key to this model is its ability to cater to a diverse audience. The digital era predominantly focuses on online content consumption, yet a significant audience segment still values physical media or requires access to content in offline settings. By offering DVDs and digital downloads, creators can effectively reach and serve this broader audience. This inclusivity in content distribution ensures that creators' works are accessible and beneficial to all viewership segments, enhancing their content's overall reach and impact.

Another pivotal aspect of this model is the enhancement of audience engagement. Offering exclusive content such as behind-the-scenes footage or special director's cut versions adds a layer of exclusivity and value. It deepens the engagement between creators and viewers, fostering a stronger, more interactive community. This enhanced engagement is beneficial for audience retention and elevates the perceived value of the content, making it more appealing for purchase.

Additionally, this approach taps into the collectibles market by transforming DVDs and digital downloads into collectible items. These products become cherished possessions for dedicated fans and collectors, especially when offered in limited editions or with unique packaging. This aspect of the business model appeals to the collector's sentiment within the fanbase, allowing fans to own a tangible piece of their favorite content.

Leveraging brand loyalty is a critical factor in the success of this model. With their established and loyal fanbases, Creators are uniquely positioned to promote and sell these products. The existing trust and connection between creators and their audience is a strong foundation for product promotion and sales. This loyalty, nurtured over time through regular content creation and interaction, can be effectively converted into a viable and profitable sales channel.

Lastly, selling stock videos as DVDs or digital downloads allows creators to adapt to market changes and opportunities. The digital content landscape is characterized by dynamism, with constantly evolving algorithms and viewer habits. By diversifying their revenue streams through physical and digital product sales, creators can navigate these changes more resiliently, ensuring a stable and diversified income source.

In essence, selling stock videos in physical and digital formats emerges as a logical and beneficial extension of the digital content creation business. It leverages existing content, meets diverse audience needs, enhances viewer engagement, taps into the collectibles market, capitalizes on brand loyalty, and provides a strategic hedge against the unpredictability of the online content market.

Monetization Through Exclusive Content

The monetization of content through exclusive elements like behind-the-scenes footage and limited edition releases represents a significant opportunity for content creators. Including exclusive BTS content is an effective strategy to attract viewers interested in the content creation process. This might encompass a range of material from outtakes and production challenges to personal anecdotes from the creators, offering a more intimate glimpse into the creative process.

Monetized

Limited edition releases, such as digital downloads or DVDs with numbered copies, create a sense of exclusivity and urgency. This approach is analogous to the director's cut or extended versions of movies, which often feature additional scenes and director commentary. Such formats have been well-received in the film industry. They can be similarly effective for YouTube content, where extended cuts or enhanced versions of popular videos are presented as unique offerings.

Creating Collectible Items for Fans

Creating collectible items for fans centers around making the product desirable and unique. Customized and branded packaging significantly enhances the appeal of these products, transforming them into sought-after collectibles, especially for loyal fans. Offering signed copies of these products can further increase their value and collectability. This strategy is reminiscent of the music industry, where limited edition signed albums are highly valued by fans. YouTube content creators can adopt a similar approach by signing a limited number of DVDs or offering special edition digital content, thereby increasing these items' perceived value and appeal.

Providing Offline Access to Content

In targeting specific audience segments, content creators can identify and cater to those who may require or prefer offline access to content. This group includes individuals in areas with limited internet access and those who have a preference for physical media. One effective tactic is to bundle digital downloads with devices with branded USB drives. This not only expands the accessibility of the content but also provides a unique value proposition to the audience.

Bundling with Additional Materials

The value of DVDs and digital downloads can be enhanced by including additional materials such as commentary tracks and tutorials. Reaction/commentary tracks, where creators discuss the content in detail, add depth and insight to the viewing experience, similar to director's commentaries in films. For example, a

Monetized

filmmaking channel might include tutorials on video editing, thereby providing additional educational value to the audience. The Criterion Collection serves as a prime case study in this regard. They release films with a plethora of bonus materials like documentaries, essays, and commentaries, significantly enriching the overall value of their offerings.

Scaling with DVD Burners

Adopting DVD burners as a core component of the implementation strategy offers a scalable and cost-effective solution for small content creators venturing into physical media sales. This approach can utilize print-on-demand inventory management and batch processing efficiencies, allowing entrepreneurs to capture the most profit.

Initially, creators can start with a print-on-demand model, using DVD burners to produce copies as orders come in. This method minimizes upfront costs and inventory risks, making it an ideal starting point for creators new to physical media sales. The low cost of DVD-burning equipment makes it a viable option even for smaller creators, allowing them to test the waters without significant financial commitment. As demand grows, scaling with automated DVD burners is a convenient and low-cost upgrade.

Additionally, leveraging software like Photoshop to design DVD menus and covers adds a professional touch to the product. Custom-designed menus and covers enhance the DVDs' aesthetic appeal and provide a branding opportunity. Creators can design unique themes that resonate with their content and brand identity, making the DVDs more appealing to fans and collectors.

This strategy effectively combines the accessibility and affordability of DVD-burning technology with the creative flexibility offered by graphic design software. It allows content creators to produce high-quality, branded physical media that appeals to their audience, all while maintaining control over production costs and scalability.

Monetized

SPONSORSHIPS AND ADVERTISEMENTS

Sponsorships and advertising represent a pivotal business model for content creators, offering a practical avenue for monetization while leveraging the creators' unique audience engagement. This model is grounded in the synergy between a creator's niche content and a sponsor's target market, allowing for a mutually beneficial relationship. Through their developed audience trust and understanding of viewer preferences, content creators provide an invaluable platform for brands to showcase their products or services.

The rationale behind sponsorships is twofold: financial stability for creators and targeted marketing for sponsors. For creators, sponsorships provide a more predictable and often substantial revenue stream than the fluctuating income from ad revenue or viewer donations. This stability enables creators to invest more time and resources into producing high-quality content, further enhancing their value to sponsors.

From a brand's perspective, sponsoring a channel offers access to a dedicated and engaged audience. Unlike traditional advertising, which can be hit or miss, sponsorships allow brands to tap into a creator's loyal following, who are likely to have a genuine interest in the brand's offerings. This targeted approach often results in higher conversion rates, making it an attractive marketing strategy.

Moreover, creators often have a deep connection with their audience, built on trust and authenticity. When a creator endorses a product, it comes across as a personal recommendation rather than a corporate advertisement. Brands highly value this level of personal endorsement, as it can significantly influence consumer behavior.

In essence, sponsorships online blend the commercial needs of brands with the creative output of content creators, all while maintaining the trust and interest of the audience. This business model supports the financial sustainability of content creation and provides value to the audience through relevant and authentic brand interactions.

Long-Term Channel Sponsorships

Long-term channel sponsorships typically involve a partnership between a brand and a channel for an extended period, ranging from several months to a year. These sponsorships can manifest in various forms, including brand mentions, product placements, or branded content segments within videos. Such collaborations provide a steady revenue stream for the creator and allow for deeper and more meaningful brand integration, benefiting both the creator and the sponsor.

To effectively harness the potential of long-term sponsorships, content creators should first identify potential sponsors whose brand values and target audience align closely with their channel's ethos and viewership. Crafting a compelling sponsorship proposal is crucial. This proposal should underscore the channel's reach, demographic details of the audience, and engagement statistics to demonstrate its potential value to the sponsor. Offering a range of sponsorship packages allows flexibility and caters to different levels of sponsor involvement and visibility, enhancing the appeal to various potential sponsors.

In the tech review space, channels often secure long-term sponsorships with gadget manufacturers or software companies, where their products are continuously featured or reviewed. Similarly, a cooking channel might establish a long-term partnership with a kitchenware brand, integrating their products into the cooking content, thereby providing practical demonstrations of the products in use.

Episode-Specific Sponsorships

Episode-specific sponsorships offer a more focused approach to brand integration. Tailored to the content of a particular video, these sponsorships can range from product reviews to discussions or narratives closely tied to the brand's product or service. This form of sponsorship allows for a direct and relevant connection between the content and the sponsor's offering, enhancing the authenticity of the brand's message.

For successful episode-specific sponsorships, creators should develop a clear plan for integrating the brand's product or service into their content naturally and engagingly. Clear communication with sponsors about the content's scope and any creative constraints is essential to maintain a successful partnership. Additionally, maintaining transparency with the audience regarding the sponsored nature of the content is vital in preserving trust and credibility.

A typical example of episode-specific sponsorships can be seen with beauty vloggers, who might partner with cosmetic brands to create makeup tutorials using their products. Gaming channels, too, frequently collaborate with game developers, providing walkthroughs or reviews of new game releases, thereby directly engaging their audience with the sponsored product in a relevant and engaging manner.

Ad Reads in Podcasts: Embracing the Radio Business Model with a Modern Twist

The ad reads during podcasts are a modern iteration of a time-tested radio business model, where sponsors pay for their products or services to be mentioned during a broadcast. This sponsorship method has evolved into a significant sales opportunity for podcasters, allowing them to monetize their content effectively while offering value to listeners and sponsors.

In the podcasting world, ad reads have resurrected the classic radio business model, adapting it to fit the digital age. Like radio, podcasters provide a captive audience but with the advantage of often being highly targeted and engaged. Listeners tend to be loyal and trust the host, making them more receptive to advertised products or services. This trust and engagement create a valuable opportunity for sponsors looking to reach specific demographics.

Monetized

One of the unique aspects of ad reads in podcasts is the opportunity for hosts to integrate them into the content using entertaining segues seamlessly. Unlike traditional radio, where ads can feel intrusive, podcast ad reads can be woven into the fabric of the episode. Hosts can use puns, humor, and storytelling to transition into the ad, making it an enjoyable part of the listener's experience. This creative approach not only enhances listener engagement but also increases the effectiveness of the ad itself. The Daily Wire has effectively demonstrated the potential for ad reads to be more than just a sponsorship opportunity but also an integral and enjoyable part of the podcast content.

To maximize the potential of ad reads, podcasters should focus on selecting sponsors that align with their audience's interests and values. They should also work on honing their delivery to make ad reads as engaging and natural as possible. This might involve scripting creative introductions or using personal anecdotes to introduce the product. The goal is to make the ad feel like a recommendation from a trusted friend rather than a commercial break.

Negotiating with Sponsors

Negotiating with sponsors and advertisers is critical for content creators seeking to monetize their platforms effectively. The process requires a strategic approach to ensure mutually beneficial outcomes for the creator and the sponsor.

Know your worth

Successful negotiation begins with a thorough understanding of your audience demographics. Knowledge of your audience's age, interests, and preferences is instrumental in demonstrating the value of your channel to potential sponsors. This detailed understanding allows you to present your platform as an ideal match for the sponsor's target market, increasing the likelihood of securing a sponsorship deal.

Monetized

Setting Clear Sponsorship Guidelines

It is essential to establish clear sponsorship guidelines. This clarity involves defining the scope of what you want to endorse or feature in your content. Setting these boundaries early helps avoid potential conflicts and ensures that any sponsorship aligns with your channel's ethos and brand values. For instance, creators focused on health and wellness might avoid partnerships with brands that contradict this theme.

Delivering Measurable Results

Using analytics to demonstrate the impact of your content is a powerful negotiation tool. Tangible metrics such as view counts, engagement rates, and audience growth often persuade potential sponsors. These statistics provide concrete evidence of your channel's reach and influence, making a compelling case for the value of partnering with your platform.

Balancing Sponsorship and Content Integrity

Maintaining a balance between sponsorships and content integrity is crucial for preserving audience trust and the authenticity of your channel.

Disclosing Sponsored Content

Transparency with your audience is paramount. Disclosing sponsored content helps maintain audience trust and complies with advertising standards. This transparency reassures viewers that you are upfront about your partnerships, helping preserve your content's integrity.

Choosing Sponsorships that Align with Your Channel

Selecting sponsorships that align with your channel's content and values is vital. This alignment ensures that sponsored content feels like a natural extension of your programming. For example, a tech

Monetized

review channel partnering with a tech company offers relevant and valuable content to its audience, maintaining the channel's focus and quality.

Retaining Creative Control

Retaining creative control over how products or services are presented in your videos is essential. This control allows you to integrate sponsored content that resonates with your audience and remains true to your style and tone. Maintaining this creative autonomy ensures that the sponsorship adds value to your content rather than detracting from it.

COMMUNITY DONATION PLATFORMS

In the evolving landscape of digital content creation, leveraging community donation platforms like Patreon represents a strategic business model for creators. This approach capitalizes on the unique relationship between creators and their audience, transforming viewer engagement into a sustainable revenue stream. The justification for adopting this model lies in its ability to directly monetize the loyalty and support of the audience, a critical asset in the content creation ecosystem.

Community donation platforms make sense for content creators as they offer direct financial support, unmediated by the constraints and fluctuations of ad revenue or sponsorships. This model provides a more stable and predictable income for long-term planning and content production. Furthermore, it enables creators to cultivate a closer relationship with their audience. By offering exclusive content, creators can enhance the value proposition for their viewers, encouraging them to transition from passive consumers to active supporters.

The audience, on their part, is often willing to support creators whose content they find valuable, entertaining, or informative. This willingness is amplified when creators offer additional exclusive benefits, fostering a sense of exclusivity and community. Platforms like Patreon are not just about financial transactions but about building a community around shared interests and providing a space for deeper interaction between creators and fans. This community-building aspect is crucial, as it leads to higher engagement, stronger loyalty, and, consequently, a more robust and supportive fan base.

Moreover, the model is grounded in transparency and rewards, vital in maintaining and growing a supporter base. Transparency in how funds are used builds trust and accountability, making supporters more inclined to continue their patronage. The offering of rewards,

Monetized

whether exclusive content, merchandise, or personal interactions, is a tangible acknowledgment of the supporters' contributions, further cementing their loyalty.

In essence, community donation platforms align the interests of content creators and their audiences, creating a symbiotic relationship where both parties benefit. Creators gain a reliable income and a dedicated fan base, while supporters receive exclusive content and a sense of belonging in a community that shares their interests. This business model is not just about financial gains; it's about fostering a community where content creators can thrive alongside their most dedicated fans.

Tiered Membership Levels

Offering tiered membership levels is a strategic approach in community donation platforms catering to diverse supporters. This system allows content creators to provide various options, each with unique benefits, appealing to different levels of engagement and financial commitment from the audience. The key is to design each tier to incrementally increase value, encouraging members to opt for higher tiers. This structure maximizes revenue potential and satisfies various audience segments, from casual supporters to the most dedicated fans.

Regular Communication

Regular communication with members keeps them engaged and invested in the community. This can be achieved through consistent updates, newsletters, or interactive community chats. Regular communication serves as a reminder of the community's value and helps build a lasting relationship between the creator and the audience. It's essential that this communication feels personal and genuine, making members feel like an integral part of the creator's journey. A better connection with the content creator is inherently part of a higher-tier subscription's value proposition and should not be overlooked.

Monetized

Exclusive Content for Members

Providing exclusive content forms a compelling value proposition for viewers to transition into paying members. It revolves around offering unique, members-only content that enhances the sense of exclusivity and special access. This approach incentivizes membership and strengthens the bond between creators and their audience, as members feel they are receiving something unique and unavailable to the general public.

Member-Only Events

Hosting exclusive events for members, such as Q&A sessions, webinars, or live chats, adds significant value to the membership experience. These events allow deeper interaction and engagement, allowing members to connect more personally with the creator and each other. Such exclusivity not only reinforces the value of the membership but also fosters a sense of community among the supporters.

Behind-the-Scenes Content

Sharing exclusive behind-the-scenes videos or personal vlogs adds a layer of intimacy and insider access, deepening the connection with the audience.

Early Access

Allowing members to access content before the general public can be a powerful incentive, making membership feel more exclusive.

Member-Only Tutorials or Webinars

Offering educational or informative sessions for members can add significant educational value to the membership, catering to those interested in more in-depth knowledge or skills.

Engaging with the Community

Active engagement with the community is a cornerstone for retaining members and fostering a sense of belonging. Effective engagement strategies should emphasize creating a reciprocal relationship where members feel heard, valued, and integral to the community. This level of interaction sustains member interest and cultivates a loyal and supportive base.

Community Polls and Feedback Sessions

Involving members in decision-making processes or seeking input on potential content topics can significantly enhance their sense of value and inclusion in the creative process. Conducting regular community polls and feedback sessions helps ensure that the content and initiatives align with the members' preferences and interests. This collaborative approach empowers members and gives creators valuable insights to refine their offerings.

Regular Engagement Posts

Utilizing community boards or posts to facilitate ongoing discussions keeps the community vibrant and engaged. Regular updates, thought-provoking questions, and interactive posts encourage members to participate actively, share their thoughts, and connect. This continuous flow of communication helps maintain a dynamic and interactive environment.

Personal Responses

Personally responding to comments or messages can significantly enhance member loyalty. When creators take the time to engage directly with their audience, it demonstrates a genuine commitment to their community. This personal touch fosters deeper connections and shows members their voices are heard and appreciated.

Monetized

Transparency and Rewards

Maintaining transparency about using funds and providing tangible rewards are crucial in enhancing supporter loyalty. Transparency builds trust and shows members the direct impact of their contributions, while rewards serve as tangible tokens of appreciation, acknowledging the support and commitment of the members.

Clear Communication on Fund Usage

Regularly updating members on how their contributions are utilized is essential for maintaining trust. Whether the funds are allocated for equipment upgrades, content improvement, or funding new projects, clear communication helps members understand the value and impact of their support. This transparency reinforces their sense of contribution to the community's growth and success.

Reward Fulfillment

Ensuring that any promised rewards are delivered promptly and are of high quality is vital in demonstrating commitment and appreciation to the members. Meeting or exceeding expectations in reward fulfillment strengthens loyalty and reinforces the creator's credibility and reliability.

Custom Rewards

Personalizing rewards based on member preferences or membership levels can significantly enhance the perceived value and personal connection to the community. Tailored rewards show that the creator recognizes and values individual contributions, fostering a more profound sense of belonging and appreciation.

SUPERCUTS AND REUSING CONTENT

Supercuts represent a strategic approach to content monetization, allowing creators to repackage existing content in an appealing and profitable format. This business model capitalizes on the vast content repository creators have already produced, transforming it into something new and engaging without needing fresh content creation. This method is particularly advantageous when generating new material, which is challenging, ensuring that the channel remains dynamic and monetarily productive.

The rationale behind supercuts lies in their ability to re-engage existing audiences and attract new viewers. By consolidating past content's most compelling, humorous, or informative segments into a cohesive video, creators can provide a condensed and enriched viewing experience. This revitalizes interest among current subscribers and serves as an accessible entry point for new audiences who might be overwhelmed by the volume of existing content.

Moreover, supercuts offer a unique opportunity for content creators to extend the lifecycle of their material. The original videos retain their standalone value, while the supercuts provide a fresh perspective, doubling the content's exposure and utility. This dual utility maximizes the return on investment for the original content creation efforts.

Supercuts can be repurposed into various formats, such as physical DVDs or digital downloads. This adaptability opens up additional revenue streams, allowing creators to reach segments of their audience who prefer physical media or downloadable content. It also caters to viewers seeking collectible items or wanting to consume content offline, further broadening the creator's market reach.

In essence, supercuts embody an intelligent fusion of creativity and commerce. They leverage the creator's existing body of work, minimize resource expenditure, and tap into various audience preferences. This model makes sense from a content creation standpoint and aligns seamlessly with audience engagement strategies, making it a potent tool in a content creator's monetization arsenal.

Creating Effective Supercuts

The first step in creating effective supercuts involves a meticulous analysis of past videos to identify themes or topics that particularly resonated with the audience. Utilizing tools like YouTube Analytics is crucial in this process, as it provides insights into which videos garnered the most engagement, views, or shares. This data-driven approach ensures that the chosen themes for supercuts align with viewer preferences, increasing the likelihood of successful re-engagement.

An essential aspect of supercuts is maintaining narrative cohesion. Ensuring a straightforward narrative or thematic link between clips is vital when compiling them. This cohesion is not just about stringing together popular segments; it's about creating a compilation that tells a story or follows a logical theme. This approach keeps viewers engaged and gives the supercut a purposeful feel rather than appearing as a random assortment of clips.

Delayed Release Schedule

Implementing a delayed release schedule for supercuts, typically six months to 1 year after the original series has concluded, can be highly effective. This timing allows the initial content to be fully monetized and gives time for a fan base to develop, which can lead to renewed interest when the long-form content is released. The strategy used by the YouTube channel Neebs Gaming exemplifies this approach, successfully remonetizing older content that might otherwise get lost in an extensive content library.

Monetized

Sponsorship Integration

Integrating sponsorships relevant to the supercut's theme presents a lucrative opportunity. For instance, a supercut of travel vlogs can attract sponsorships from travel gear companies. These compilations are more marketable as their content popularity and quality are already established, offering a safer investment for potential sponsors.

YouTube Ads

The extended length of supercuts makes them ideal candidates for multiple ad placements. This increased ad space can significantly boost potential ad revenue, turning longer viewing times into a financial advantage for the content creator.

Exclusive Access via Patreon

Offering early or exclusive access to supercuts to Patreon supporters adds significant value to membership. This strategy incentivizes viewers to become paying members and provides them with exclusivity and appreciation for their support.

Seasonal or Event-based Themes

Creating supercuts based on seasonal events or current trends can make the content more relevant and engaging. For example, compiling all Halloween or Christmas-themed episodes caters to viewers' seasonal interests and can attract a dedicated audience during specific times of the year.

Collaborations for Themed Supercuts

Collaborating with other creators to compile themed content can significantly expand the reach of a supercut. These collaborations can introduce creators to new audiences, foster community within the creator space, and add variety to the compiled content. Consider

Monetized

having a trusted colleague react with the content creator as additional/fresh content to draw attention to the recycled content.

Editing Efficiency

Given that most of the content for supercuts has already been created, the editing process involves a relatively simple workflow. Proficiency in editing software is still necessary to ensure the final product is polished and professionally presented.

SEO Optimization

Optimizing the supercut's title, description, and tags for search engines is critical for increasing its visibility. Employing strategic titles like "The Movie" can capture the essence of the compilation and attract more viewers through search engine results and YouTube recommendations. This SEO optimization ensures that the supercut reaches the broadest possible audience.

EXPAND SOCIAL MEDIA PRESENCE

Expanding social media presence has become a critical strategy for content creators in the digital era, where content consumption is not limited to a single platform. This approach is rooted in the understanding that different social media platforms cater to diverse audience demographics, each with unique content preferences and engagement patterns. For instance, platforms like Instagram and TikTok attract a predominantly younger audience that favors visually driven and short-form content. At the same time, LinkedIn and Twitter appeal to more mature, professionally-oriented users.

Leveraging multiple platforms allows content creators to tap into these varied audience pools, extending their reach to potential subscribers. This expanded reach is not just about numbers; it's about diversifying the audience base, increasing the potential for higher engagement, and widening the scope for monetization. A presence across multiple platforms ensures that a creator's content and brand are visible in more places, capturing the attention of audiences who might not be regular YouTube or Twitch users but are active on other social media channels.

The rationale behind using social media as sales funnels to more profitable monetization channels is grounded in accessibility and convenience. Social media platforms offer an immediate and interactive way for creators to connect with their audience, share updates, and direct traffic to their monetization channels, such as online stores, Patreon accounts, or affiliate links. This direct line to monetization avenues is crucial in the digital content creation, where the journey from viewer to customer or patron can be as short as a click.

Furthermore, consistent branding across all platforms reinforces a creator's identity and message, which is vital for building a strong, recognizable brand. In a crowded digital landscape, a cohesive brand image and messaging help establish trust and reliability with the audience, making them more likely to engage with the content and follow through on monetization channels.

In summary, expanding social media presence aligns perfectly with the business model of content creators. It amplifies their reach, diversifies their audience, and strategically positions them to capitalize on various monetization opportunities. Leveraging the audience across different platforms becomes a key driver for success, ensuring that content creators maximize their potential in the digital marketplace.

Platform-Specific Content

Understanding and respecting the unique characteristics of each social media platform is essential for content creators. Tailoring content to suit the format and audience of each platform enhances engagement and relevance. For example, Instagram thrives on short-form, visually compelling content, making it an ideal platform for visually rich posts and stories. Conversely, LinkedIn caters to a professional audience, making it more suitable for informative, article-style content that offers value in a business context. Adapting to each platform's strengths allows creators to effectively communicate their message and engage with different audience segments in the most appropriate and impactful way.

Cross-Promotion

Cross-promotion is a strategic approach to expand reach and audience engagement across different platforms. By using each platform to promote content to others, creators can drive traffic and increase viewership on all their channels. For instance, announcing a new YouTube video on Twitter or highlighting an upcoming Instagram Live session on Facebook can attract audiences from one platform to another. This interconnected promotion creates a web of content, encouraging followers to engage with the creator's content across multiple platforms, amplifying the overall reach and impact.

Monetized

Engagement Tactics

Engaging regularly with the audience is crucial for building a robust and loyal community. Interaction through comments, live sessions, and stories fosters a sense of connection and community among followers. These tactics enhance audience engagement and provide valuable feedback and insights into audience preferences and behavior. Active engagement helps create a more personalized experience for the audience, making them feel valued and part of the creator's journey.

Thor from Pirate Software, who experienced significant growth by uploading Twitch content onto YouTube, particularly YouTube Shorts, is an example of successful cross-platform engagement. This strategy effectively tapped into different audience preferences, showcasing the power of platform-specific content and cross-promotion.

Sales Funnels to Monetization Channels

Social media platforms are invaluable in guiding followers towards various monetization channels. By strategically using these platforms, creators can convert followers into paying customers or supporters.

Direct links in bios and posts make it easy for followers to navigate to monetization platforms like merchandise stores or Patreon pages. Exclusive offers announced on social media can create a sense of urgency and exclusivity, encouraging followers to take immediate action. Collaborating with other influencers can broaden reach and introduce the creator's content to new audiences, further driving traffic to monetization channels.

Consistent Branding Across Platforms

Maintaining consistent branding across all social media platforms is crucial in building brand recognition and credibility. This consistency ensures that the audience immediately identifies and connects with the creator's content, regardless of the platform.

Monetized

Unified visual identity should be consistent across all platforms, including logo, color scheme, and typography. The tone, messaging, and content themes should be coherent, reflecting the creator's brand and values in every post and interaction. Developing branding guidelines helps maintain this consistency.

Creators can use tools like Canva or Adobe Spark to create consistent visual elements. Implementing a content calendar aids in planning and ensuring consistent messaging and branding across all platforms. Gathering audience feedback helps understand how the audience perceives the brand across different platforms, allowing for necessary adjustments.

A notable example of consistent branding is Wendy's fast-food chain, known for its consistent, edgy, and humorous tone across Twitter, Facebook, and Instagram. This approach has made Wendy's social media presence distinct and instantly recognizable, demonstrating the effectiveness of consistent branding.

PODCASTING

Podcasting has emerged as a powerful medium for content creators looking to diversify their monetization strategies. By starting a podcast, creators can repurpose existing content, distribute it across various media channels, and reach new and diverse audiences. This chapter explores why podcasting is an effective monetization method and provides a step-by-step guide on starting a podcast.

Why Podcasting?

Podcasting offers several advantages that make it an attractive addition to a content creator's monetization toolkit. One of the primary benefits is its accessibility and convenience. Podcasts are easily accessible and can be consumed on the go, allowing creators to reach listeners who prefer audio content over visual or written formats. This convenience opens up a new avenue for engaging with audiences during their daily commutes, workouts, or downtime.

Another significant advantage is audience expansion. By tapping into the podcasting audience, creators can reach new demographics who may not engage with their content on other platforms. This expansion can increase brand recognition and a more extensive fan base. Additionally, podcasting allows for content repurposing. Creators can reuse and repurpose existing content, such as blog posts, videos, or social media discussions, which saves time and maximizes the content's value.

Moreover, podcasting offers diversified revenue streams. Podcasts can be monetized through various methods, including sponsorships, advertisements, premium content subscriptions, and listener donations. This diversity in monetization options provides creators with multiple ways to generate income. Finally, podcasting excels in community building. The conversational tone and regular episodes foster a sense of intimacy and connection between creators and their audience, helping to build a loyal and engaged community.

Standard formats include solo shows, interviews, panel discussions, and narrative storytelling. Plan the structure of each episode, including the introduction, main content, and conclusion. Consistency in structure helps listeners know what to expect. Additionally, outline your content plan, including topics for the first few episodes. Consider how you can repurpose existing content from other platforms and plan for a mix of evergreen content (timeless topics) and timely content (current events or trends).

Recording Your Podcast

Investing in the right equipment and software is essential for a successful podcast. A good quality microphone and headphones are crucial for retaining listeners through clear and professional-sounding audio. Choose recording software that suits your needs and budget. Popular options include Audacity (free), Adobe Audition (paid), and GarageBand (for Mac users).

Record in a quiet space with minimal background noise. Soundproofing materials should be used if necessary to improve audio quality. Test your equipment and do a few trial recordings to ensure everything works correctly. When recording, speak clearly and at a steady pace. Practice good microphone techniques, such as maintaining a consistent distance from the mic. Edit your recordings to remove mistakes, awkward pauses, or background noise. Adding intros, outros, and music can enhance the listening experience.

Publishing and Distributing Your Podcast

Choose a podcast hosting platform to upload and distribute your episodes. Popular options include Libsyn, Podbean, and Anchor. Ensure your hosting platform provides analytics to track your podcast's performance. Set up an RSS feed through your hosting

Monetized

platform; this feed automatically allows your podcast to be distributed to various directories.

Submit your podcast to significant directories like Apple, Spotify, Google, and Stitcher. Being on multiple platforms increases your reach. Create detailed show notes for each episode, including key points, links, and any additional resources mentioned. This helps with SEO and provides value to your listeners. Consider providing transcripts for accessibility and to reach a wider audience, including those who prefer reading.

Promoting Your Podcast

Promoting your podcast is essential for building an audience. Use your existing social media channels to promote your episodes. Engaging visuals, snippets, and teasers can attract attention and encourage sharing. Cross-promote your podcast on other platforms, such as your YouTube channel, blog, or email newsletter.

Invite guests who can bring value to your audience and expand your reach. Their followers may become your new listeners. Additionally, appear as a guest on other podcasts in your niche to tap into their audience and increase your visibility. Encourage listeners to subscribe, leave reviews, and share your podcast. Engaging with your audience helps build a loyal community. Consider creating a dedicated website or landing page for your podcast, where listeners can find all episodes, show notes, and additional resources.

ADD LANGUAGES

Expanding the reach of content across linguistic boundaries is not just an opportunity; it's a strategic necessity. The essence of this business model lies in its capacity to transform a single-content approach into a globally accessible asset. This strategy makes sense for content creators because it directly aligns with the core objectives of audience expansion, increased engagement, and diversified revenue streams.

The rationale for adding languages to content, mainly through AI-assisted translations, subtitles, and dubbing, is rooted in non-English-speaking markets' vast, untapped potential. These markets, rich in cultural diversity and viewer engagement, present a unique opportunity for creators to grow their audience exponentially. By breaking the language barrier, creators can access millions of potential viewers who were previously unreachable. This is not just about increasing numbers; it's about cultivating a global community around the content, leading to higher viewer retention and loyalty.

Moreover, this business model leverages the audience for success in several ways. Firstly, it taps into the global nature of the internet, turning what was once a local or niche audience into a worldwide one. Secondly, it respects and acknowledges the diversity of the audience, which can enhance the creator's brand perception and trustworthiness. This inclusivity fosters a deeper connection between the creator and their audience.

In addition, using AI-assisted translation and subtitle generation tools presents a cost-effective and efficient solution, making this strategy accessible even to creators with limited resources. This technological approach ensures that expanding into multiple languages is feasible and scalable as the channel grows.

Monetized

Lastly, the strategy aligns perfectly with the trend of content consumption in non-English speaking countries, where there is a growing appetite for diverse and international content. By localizing content in different languages, creators expand their audience and position themselves favorably in a competitive market where personalized and accessible content is king.

In summary, adding languages to YouTube content is a strategic move that aligns with the core goals of audience expansion, engagement, and revenue diversification. It leverages the internet's global reach, acknowledges audience diversity, and uses efficient technology to make global engagement a practical reality for creators.

AI Translation Tools

Utilizing AI translation tools like Google's AI translation or specialized services is a cornerstone in expanding content reach. These tools provide a practical and efficient means to translate video scripts into multiple languages, enabling creators to cater to a diverse global audience. The advantage of using AI tools lies in their ability to quickly handle large volumes of content, a critical factor for creators with extensive video libraries. However, the effectiveness of these translations hinges on their accuracy and relevance, which leads to the need for regular oversight and refinement.

Optimizing for Accuracy

The key to successful translation is linguistic accuracy and cultural relevance. AI translations, while efficient, can sometimes miss the nuances of cultural context and colloquialisms. Regularly reviewing and adjusting these translations is essential to maintain the integrity and relatability of the content. This process might involve working with native speakers or language experts to ensure that translations are grammatically correct and culturally resonant. Such attention to detail can significantly enhance the viewer's experience and engagement with the content.

Monetized

Keyword Optimization in Different Languages

Adapting search engine optimization (SEO) strategies to include keywords relevant to different languages is crucial for enhancing content discoverability in non-English speaking markets. This involves researching and incorporating keywords that resonate with the target audience in their native language. Such optimization ensures the content reaches the intended audience through search engines and YouTube recommendations, increasing visibility and viewership.

Channels like 'Kurzgesagt – In a Nutshell' exemplify the success of this strategy. They have significantly broadened their audience base and engagement levels by offering content in multiple languages. Additionally, the popularity of Japanese illustrated stories in the USA underscores the potential of translated content to cross cultural barriers and appeal to diverse audience groups.

Access to Non-English Speaking Audiences

Tapping into non-English speaking markets like China, India, and Latin America can open new avenues for growth, sponsorships, and revenue streams. These markets represent a vast audience with diverse preferences and interests. To effectively penetrate these markets, it's crucial to understand their unique cultural and linguistic landscapes. This understanding can be achieved through targeted market research, collaboration with native speakers, and localized marketing strategies. Such an approach ensures the content is linguistically and culturally tailored to the audience.

'TED Talks' is a prime example of a platform that has expanded its global reach through multilingual content. By offering talks in various languages, they have increased their worldwide impact and accessibility. The use of volunteer translators ensures the translations are not only accurate but also culturally relevant.

Monetized

Subtitles and Dubbing Options

The decision between subtitles and dubbing depends mainly on the content type and audience preference. Subtitles offer a straightforward way to make content accessible to non-native speakers, while dubbing provides a more immersive experience. Both methods have their place in a content creator's strategy, and the choice should be informed by the content's nature and the target audience's preferences.

Integrating subtitles using YouTube's features is a practical starting point. Engaging the community in contributing to subtitle accuracy can enhance the quality of translations. For high-value or narrative-driven content, professional dubbing services can offer a more engaging experience for viewers. Regularly soliciting audience feedback can provide insights into their preferences, guiding the creator in choosing the most effective translation method.

A phased approach to implementing subtitles and dubbing is advisable. Starting with a few languages and expanding based on viewer response and analytics allows for a more measured and effective strategy. Monitoring engagement metrics provides valuable feedback on the impact of these translation methods on viewer engagement.

Netflix's global strategy of offering multi-language subtitles and dubbing has been a critical factor in its success in penetrating international markets. Similarly, the educational channel 'Extra Credits' has increased its reach and inclusivity by offering content with subtitles in multiple languages sourced from the community. These examples highlight the effectiveness of a well-implemented language addition strategy in expanding a content creator's global footprint.

EDUCATIONAL AND INFORMATIONAL CONTENT

Educational and informative channels, ranging from academic subjects and science to business, finance, and historical explorations, cater to an audience seeking knowledge, expertise, and valuable insights. Unlike entertainment or lifestyle channels, the content here is driven by information and education, often appealing to a more niche but highly engaged audience. This chapter delves into tailored monetization strategies for creators in this segment, focusing on leveraging their specialized knowledge and audience trust.

The market for educational and informative content online is both diverse and dynamic. Many viewers turn to these channels for self-improvement, learning new skills, keeping abreast of current events, and satisfying their curiosity about the world. This trend is bolstered by an increasing preference for digital learning platforms and the accessibility of expert knowledge in various fields. Content creators in this domain often possess high expertise, credibility, and authority in their respective niches, setting them apart from other genres on YouTube.

However, monetizing educational and informative content requires a different approach than other YouTube categories. The audience here is generally more discerning and values depth, accuracy, and reliability over entertainment. They are willing to invest in their education and personal development, presenting unique opportunities for creators to monetize their content effectively. The strategies discussed in this chapter — from online courses and workshops to writing books, public speaking engagements, consulting services, and webinars — are designed to capitalize on the creator's expertise and the audience's willingness to learn.

In this competitive space, a successful monetization strategy also involves a keen understanding of market demands, audience preferences, and the latest trends in digital education. It's about creating value beyond the YouTube platform, offering in-depth knowledge and personalized experiences that viewers are willing to pay for. Each section in this chapter will explore these strategies in detail, providing insights into how educational and informative content creators can transform their passion and knowledge into a sustainable and profitable business model.

By the end of this chapter, you will clearly understand the unique opportunities and challenges of monetizing educational and informative content online and how to leverage your expertise to build a thriving online presence strategically.

ONLINE COURSES

Expertise in a particular field is a treasure trove of opportunity. This expertise, cultivated over time, can be transformed into educational content, offering in-depth insights or unique perspectives. The fundamental strategy is to identify and focus on aspects of knowledge and experience that are unique or not widely available. For instance, a YouTuber with a background in digital marketing might create a specialized course on "Advanced SEO Strategies for E-commerce," tapping into the demand for advanced knowledge in this niche. To implement this effectively, conducting market research to align the course content with the audience's needs is crucial. This is followed by creating a structured curriculum that progressively builds on the topics, ensuring a coherent and comprehensive learning journey.

Interactive Learning

Integrating interactive elements in online courses can significantly enhance learner engagement and knowledge retention. Strategies for interactive learning include incorporating quizzes, interactive assignments, or live Q&A sessions into the course structure. These elements provide immediate feedback and keep learners actively engaged. A real-world example of this can be seen in platforms like Codecademy, where coding exercises are integrated directly into the learning process, allowing for the practical application of theoretical knowledge. Content creators should regularly integrate interactive elements throughout their courses to implement this. They should also explore and utilize platforms that support these interactive features or consider third-party tools that can be seamlessly embedded into the course.

Monetized

Recurring Revenue

A subscription model in online courses provides a steady income stream and motivates content creators to update and improve their offerings continuously. The strategy involves offering courses under a subscription model, where new content is added regularly. An example of this model's success is seen in MasterClass, where members gain access to a wide range of courses for a subscription fee. Implementing this requires designing a series of logically grouped courses that offer individual value and encourage learners to continue with subsequent classes, thus sustaining their subscriptions.

Scalable Content

Scalability is crucial for maximizing the revenue potential of online courses. Once created, these courses can continually generate income with minimal additional effort. The strategy here is to create evergreen content that remains relevant over time, avoiding topics that may quickly become outdated. Courses that teach fundamental skills, such as photography or basic programming, often stay relevant and in demand, exemplifying scalable content. To implement this, content creators should focus on creating high-quality, timeless content and consider periodically updating the courses to maintain relevance and appeal.

Platform Choices

The choice of platform for hosting online courses can significantly impact their reach and profitability. While platforms like Udemy or Coursera offer a diverse audience reach and take a portion of the revenue, hosting courses independently allows for more control over content and pricing but requires more outstanding marketing efforts. For example, a tech YouTuber might initially use a platform like Udemy to capitalize on its broad audience base and then transition to its platform once they have established a solid follower base. Implementing this strategy effectively involves starting with established platforms to leverage their audience and then gradually transitioning to a personal platform using tools like Teachable or Thinkific as the brand grows.

Monetized

Tailored Content

Tailoring content to meet the audience's needs or interests increases the course's value and appeal. This involves gathering feedback from the audience to understand their learning needs and creating courses directly aligned with these interests. For instance, a cooking channel might develop a series of workshops on specific cuisines based on audience polls, directly catering to the audience's interests. Regular engagement with the audience through comments, polls, or surveys is essential to implement this. This feedback should then guide the development of courses and workshops, ensuring they align closely with the audience's interests and needs.

WRITING AND PUBLISHING A BOOK

Content creators are uniquely positioned to leverage their existing audience and expertise into book publishing. The decision to write and publish a book aligns with a strategic business model that extends beyond the confines of digital content creation, offering a tangible product that can serve as a testament to their authority and knowledge in their respective fields.

The core rationale behind this business model lies in the inherent credibility that a published book confers. Unlike transient digital content, a book is often perceived as a more substantial and enduring artifact of expertise. For content creators, this solidifies their status as authorities in their niche and provides a platform to delve deeper into subjects they are passionate about, offering their audience a more comprehensive and nuanced exploration than what is typically feasible in video format.

Moreover, this venture into book publishing opens up diversified income streams. Beyond the direct revenue from book sales, it often paves the way for ancillary opportunities such as paid speaking engagements, workshops, and consulting services, which can significantly enhance a content creator's earning potential. This diversification is particularly crucial in an ecosystem where digital ad revenues can be unpredictable and subject to the vagaries of platform algorithms.

Another compelling aspect of this model is the opportunity for cross-promotion. Content creators can leverage their platform to promote their books, accessing an engaged and loyal audience. Conversely, the book can attract new followers to its digital content, creating a synergistic relationship that boosts visibility and reach across both mediums.

Monetized

Additionally, the advent of self-publishing platforms like Amazon's Kindle Direct Publishing has democratized the publishing process, allowing creators to maintain greater control over their content, retain higher royalties, and respond more agilely to market demands. This control is particularly appealing in a landscape where traditional publishing routes can be fraught with barriers to entry and creative constraints.

In summary, writing and publishing a book offers content creators a multifaceted opportunity to expand their brand, establish authority, diversify income, and deepen their connection with their audience. This business model makes sense from a financial standpoint and enhances the creator's influence and reach, both online and in the broader realm of their industry.

Establishing Authority

In the digital age, book authoring remains a revered benchmark of expertise and depth of knowledge. This traditional symbol of authority allows content creators to delve deeply into their subjects, offering a level of exploration and detail that often surpasses what can be conveyed through videos or series. The critical strategy lies in identifying gaps in existing literature and focusing on unique insights or perspectives that the content creator can offer. Implementing this involves starting with an outline of chapters based on popular content and then expanding these with thorough research and unique viewpoints, crafting a narrative that resonates with the audience while establishing the author's authority in the field.

Diversified Income

Publishing a book opens up multiple streams of income for content creators. Beyond the direct sales of the book, an enhanced profile can lead to lucrative opportunities like speaking engagements and workshops. Strategic pricing of the book is crucial, balancing volume sales against high-margin sales. To effectively implement this, creators should network with event organizers and offer their book as part of speaking engagement contracts, thereby integrating the book into a broader income-generating strategy.

Monetized

Cross-Promotion

For content creators, their existing platform is an invaluable tool for promoting their books. The trust and rapport already established with their audience make them potential buyers. The strategy here is to create content that complements the book's topics, include book excerpts in videos, and engage in interactive Q&A sessions about the book. Implementing this involves planning a content schedule encompassing book teasers, behind-the-scenes glimpses of the writing process, and launch countdowns, effectively harnessing the synergy between the book and the digital platform.

Wide Distribution

Maximizing the book's reach necessitates accessibility. Different audience segments have varied preferences, some favoring physical copies and others leaning toward digital formats. The strategy involves utilizing print-on-demand services to minimize upfront costs for physical copies and distributing digital copies across multiple platforms. Implementation requires partnering with online distributors for digital formats and using services like Amazon's CreateSpace for physical copies, ensuring the book is accessible to a broad spectrum of readers.

Self-Publishing Options

Self-publishing offers creators control over their content and the potential for higher royalties compared to traditional publishing routes. The restrictive nature and often lower traditional publishing royalties make self-publishing an attractive alternative. Strategies include using platforms like Amazon's Kindle Direct Publishing for e-books and print-on-demand services. A notable case study is E.L. James' "Fifty Shades of Grey," which began as a self-published piece before becoming a global sensation. Implementation involves learning the basics of self-publishing, producing a quality manuscript, and employing professional services for editing, cover design, and formatting to ensure a polished final product.

Monetized

Collaborative Writing

Collaboration in writing can amalgamate diverse expertise and extend the book's audience reach. Co-authoring with another expert in a related field can significantly enhance the book's credibility and appeal. The strategy is to identify experts whose audience complements the creator's, ensuring an applicable audience. An example of successful collaborative writing is "Freakonomics" by Stephen J. Dubner and Steven Levitt, which merged economics with storytelling to appeal to a broad audience. To implement this, creators should network to find potential co-authors, establish a shared vision, and clearly define roles and responsibilities, ensuring a cohesive and effective collaborative effort.

PUBLIC SPEAKING ENGAGEMENTS

Integrating public speaking engagements into a content creator's business model offers a strategic pathway to elevate their brand and expand their influence. This approach leverages the creator's established audience and expertise, branching from the digital realm to more traditional, high-impact platforms.

Public speaking engagements are a natural extension for extroverted content creators. Their online presence provides a foundational audience base and establishes them as subject matter experts. Engaging with audiences in a live, in-person setting or through virtual conferences allows for a more dynamic interaction. This direct connection reinforces the creator's authority in their field and enhances their brand visibility beyond their digital footprint.

The rationale behind pursuing public speaking opportunities lies in the multifaceted benefits they offer. Firstly, the events can be recorded and edited to become content themselves, letting the content creator double dip on their efforts. Next, these engagements serve as an effective brand-building tool. Being a keynote speaker or a panelist at reputable events positions the creator as a thought leader, lending credibility and prestige to their online persona. This recognition can lead to increased viewership and subscriber growth on their channels.

Secondly, the networking aspect of public speaking engagements cannot be overstated. These events often gather like-minded individuals, industry professionals, and potential collaborators, opening doors to new opportunities, partnerships, and cross-promotional activities. Such networking can create collaborative content, expand audience reach, and diversify the creator's content.

Moreover, public speaking offers a tangible revenue stream. Once established, creators can command speaking fees, providing a direct and often lucrative source of income. This revenue diversification is crucial for creators looking to build a sustainable financial model in the often fluctuating world of online content creation.

Lastly, audience interaction in public speaking engagements provides invaluable feedback and insights. Understanding audience reactions, questions, and discussions can inform future content creation, ensuring it remains relevant and engaging. This feedback loop creates a deeper connection with the audience, fostering a loyal community around the creator's brand.

Building Personal Brand

Public speaking in conferences and events establishes creators as authorities in their respective fields, significantly enhancing their reputation and credibility. The exposure gained from these prominent platforms elevates the creator's status, setting them apart from competitors. To capitalize on this, creators should strategically select speaking opportunities that align with their brand and content. This involves tailoring talks to showcase unique insights and expertise, ensuring they resonate with the creator's existing content. By crafting signature talks that offer deeper insights or address complementary topics, creators can reinforce their brand identity and expertise, attracting a wider audience and enhancing their overall market presence.

Networking Opportunities

Engagements in public speaking provide an invaluable platform for creators to connect with peers, industry leaders, and potential collaborators. These interactions are instrumental in opening doors to collaborative projects, cross-promotion opportunities, and a broader audience reach. To maximize these benefits, creators should actively engage in networking sessions during these events, initiating conversations and exchanging contact information. The follow-up post-event is equally crucial in cementing these new relationships. Proactive participation in networking sessions and setting up meetings with key individuals in advance can lead to valuable collaborations and partnerships, as evidenced by many successful YouTubers.

Paid Engagements

For seasoned speakers, public speaking engagements can become a significant source of revenue. This model compensates for the time and effort invested in preparing and delivering talks. Creators are advised to start with smaller, possibly unpaid gigs to build a speaking portfolio and then progressively seek higher-paying opportunities as their reputation grows—network with your local community college or other higher education organizations to start. Clearly defining speaking rates and negotiating terms that reflect the creator's growing stature and audience reach is crucial in establishing a sustainable revenue stream from public speaking engagements.

Speaker Agencies

Speaker agencies play a critical role in securing speaking opportunities for content creators. With their expertise and extensive networks, these agencies can place creators in high-profile events, often negotiating better rates and terms. For creators, joining a reputable speaker agency that aligns with their content domain is a strategic move. Preparing a compelling speaker profile and a reel of past speaking engagements is essential to attract top agencies. Case studies show that many successful public speakers rely on agencies to manage their speaking careers efficiently, focusing on content creation while the agency handles logistics and negotiations.

Workshop Integration

Integrating workshops with speaking engagements adds significant value for the audience. These workshops offer a platform for deeper engagement and can serve as an additional revenue stream. Creators should develop workshops that complement their speaking topics, providing hands-on experiences or in-depth learning opportunities. This integration enhances the value of the speaking engagement and strengthens the creator's brand as a comprehensive knowledge provider. Effective planning and marketing of these workshops,

Monetized speaking engagements, and offering special rates or exclusive content for attendees can significantly increase participation and audience engagement.

Audience Interaction

Direct interaction with the audience during speaking events offers content creators valuable insights and feedback. This engagement is critical in understanding the audience's needs and preferences, shaping future content creation, and building a stronger community around the creator's brand. Incorporating interactive elements like Q&A sessions, live polls, and feedback forms makes these engagements more dynamic and informative. The insights gained from these interactions should be actively used to inform the creator's content strategy, ensuring it remains relevant, engaging, and aligned with audience interests. This ongoing dialogue between the creator and the audience fosters community and keeps the content fresh and responsive to viewer needs.

CONSULTING SERVICES

Consulting services can be a lucrative and strategic business model for content creators, especially those in the educational and informative sector who have established themselves as experts. The rationale behind this model hinges on several key factors that align with the strengths and opportunities inherent in content creation.

Content creation establishes the channel as an authority in their respective niches. Through consistent content delivery, they have demonstrated expertise and garnered trust from their audience. This established credibility is a cornerstone for consulting, as clients seek advisors knowledgeable and trusted by a broader community.

Secondly, the audience base of a channel is a rich resource. These viewers are not just passive consumers; they often actively seek solutions and insights related to the channel's content. By transitioning from general content delivery to personalized consulting, creators can address specific audience needs more directly and effectively. This transition from a one-to-many to a one-on-one interaction allows for deeper engagement and can lead to more impactful outcomes.

Moreover, the diversity and size of an audience provide a vast potential client base. Among viewers, there are likely individuals and organizations facing challenges or seeking improvements in areas where the content creator has proven expertise. Thus, the audience cultivated through YouTube can be seamlessly leveraged into a consulting clientele.

The digital nature of content creation also plays a crucial role. Familiarity with online tools, digital communication, and content management usage generally means that creators can efficiently handle the logistics of online consulting. This expertise enables them

Monetized

to offer flexible, accessible, and scalable consulting services, reaching clients globally without geographical constraints.

Finally, consulting services offer content creators a sustainable and scalable revenue model. Unlike ad revenues or sponsorships, which fluctuate, consulting can provide a more stable income, primarily when structured as retainer services or long-term contracts. This stability is vital for content creators looking to diversify their income streams and build a more resilient business model.

One-on-One Sessions

Personalized consulting, characterized by one-on-one sessions, enables a deep and focused exploration of the unique challenges faced by individual clients. This approach often leads to more effective solutions than generalized advice, allowing the consultant to tailor their expertise to the client's needs and context.

The key to effective one-on-one consulting is understanding and identifying the common pain points within your niche. You can strategically position your consulting services to address these challenges by recognizing them. Utilizing tools like Calendly simplifies the scheduling process, while platforms like Zoom facilitate a personal connection despite geographical barriers.

It is common for fitness content creators to transition into personal fitness consulting. By focusing on individualized fitness plans and nutritional advice, they were able to increase their revenue. This shift boosts their income and enhances their reputation as a personalized fitness expert.

Retainer Services

Retainer services provide a consistent revenue stream and foster ongoing relationships with clients. This setup is beneficial as it offers a sense of security for both the consultant and the client, with the client receiving continuous support and securing a stable income.

Monetized

It's essential to develop a range of packages that cater to different levels of client needs and budgets. These could be based on the number of hours of consultancy provided or specific services offered. Communicating the advantages of ongoing support over one-time consultations can help convince potential clients of the value of a retainer agreement.

Corporate Consulting

Corporate consulting is particularly lucrative due to the larger budgets and more comprehensive needs of corporate clients. These clients often seek extensive, ongoing consulting engagements, which can provide significant income and professional growth opportunities for content creators.

Success in corporate consulting hinges on offering comprehensive, customized packages that meet corporate clients' broad and often complex needs. Networking is crucial in this arena. Utilizing platforms like LinkedIn and attending relevant industry events can be effective strategies for connecting with potential corporate clients.

Online Consultations

The digital age has made online consultations a viable and efficient method to reach a global audience. This approach allows content creators to extend their consulting services beyond local boundaries, tapping into a wider pool of potential clients.

To offer effective online consultations, it's crucial to use reliable video conferencing tools that ensure clear communication and a good user experience. Additionally, offering flexible scheduling to accommodate different time zones can significantly enhance accessibility for a global clientele.

Customized Solutions

Offering customized solutions is essential in consulting, ensuring the services provided are directly relevant and valuable to the client.

Monetized

This approach leads to higher client satisfaction and often results in longer-term engagements.

Developing customized solutions requires a thorough initial assessment to understand each client's needs and challenges. Building a portfolio that showcases your ability to solve diverse problems can be a persuasive tool in attracting new clients.

WEBINARS

Webinars provide a unique opportunity for creators to showcase their expertise. This approach establishes them as thought leaders in their respective fields and attracts an audience that seeks more in-depth knowledge. The fundamental strategy here involves identifying niche topics that resonate with your existing audience, which can be discerned using YouTube analytics. The implementation of these sessions requires an explicit curriculum, strategic advertising on YouTube and social media platforms, and the utilization of efficient webinar platforms like Zoom or Webex to host these expert sessions.

Interactive Format

An interactive format is crucial in enhancing the webinar experience, as it keeps the audience actively engaged and provides a richer learning experience. This interactive approach increases audience satisfaction and ensures higher retention rates. Successful strategies for interactive webinars include planning for Q&A sessions, utilizing polls to gauge audience opinions, and fostering real-time discussions. A notable case study in this regard is TED-Ed, known for its interactive webinars that often include audience polls and Q&A segments, significantly enhancing viewer engagement. To successfully implement this, creators must prepare interactive elements well in advance and ensure the chosen webinar tools are tested and ready for smooth execution.

Collaborations

Collaborating with other experts in the field can significantly broaden the scope of the webinar content while attracting diverse audience bases. Such collaborations bring varied perspectives and enhance the webinar's credibility and appeal. The strategy here involves identifying and reaching out to potential collaborators

Monetized

whose expertise complements your own. Implementing this strategy requires careful coordination of content, logistics, and joint promotional efforts to ensure the success of the collaborative webinar.

Monetization Options

Offering webinars for free with the option for paid upgrades is an effective model to cater to a large audience while providing additional value for those willing to pay. This model, as seen in the case of companies like HubSpot, often offers free webinars with options to purchase advanced training sessions, attracts viewers with the allure of free content, and then offers more in-depth material for a fee. Implementing this monetization strategy involves providing primary access to webinars for free, with additional paid upgrades such as extended materials, personalized one-on-one sessions, or access to a series of webinars. A critical aspect of this approach is setting up a reliable payment gateway and clear communication of the benefits associated with the paid upgrade.

Recorded Access

Providing recorded versions of webinars can significantly extend the reach of the content, allowing individuals to access it at their convenience. This approach efficiently caters to a global audience, which might be spread across various time zones. The strategy involves recording the webinars and offering them for individual purchase or as part of a subscription model. Ensuring high-quality recordings and securing a reliable platform for distributing and selling these recordings is essential for successfully implementing this strategy.

Feedback Mechanism

Utilizing webinars to obtain feedback is an effective way to tailor content to audience needs. Direct feedback from the audience provides valuable insights into their preferences and highlights potential gaps in content. The strategy involves including feedback forms at the end of webinars and encouraging live feedback during the session. This feedback should then be integrated into future content planning. Implementing this mechanism requires the integration of feedback forms into the webinar platform and a thorough analysis of the responses to inform content improvement.

Technical Considerations and Iterative Process

For YouTube content creators and streamers, the transition to hosting webinars is often straightforward, given that most already possess the equipment and software for live streaming. OBS Studio or Streamyard are ideal for streaming, while platforms like Zoom or GoToWebinar are excellent for hosting interactive webinars. Ensuring reliable internet connectivity, good audio quality, and a distraction-free environment is critical. Creators should adopt an iterative process, starting with shorter, simpler webinars to gauge audience interest and gradually expanding to more complex topics based on feedback and engagement metrics. This approach allows creators to refine their webinar hosting skills and content relevance.

CREATIVE AND ARTISTIC CHANNELS

Creative and artistic channels range from visual and design to music and culinary arts. They entertain and inspire and provide a platform for creators to showcase their talents. This chapter delves into the distinctive monetization strategies tailored for such channels, focusing on how artists and creatives can transform their passion into a sustainable livelihood.

Creative and artistic channels differ significantly from other genres in their emotional and personal connection with the audience. These channels often showcase the creative process, providing a behind-the-scenes look at creating art, music, and other forms of creative expression. This transparency and authenticity foster a robust, engaged community eager to support the creator's journey.

The digital era has revolutionized the way art and creative content are consumed. With the rise of social media and online platforms, there is a growing demand for unique, personalized content. This shift has opened up new avenues for monetization, especially for artists and creatives who traditionally relied on galleries or physical venues. The digital marketplace provides greater accessibility and reach, allowing creators to connect with a global audience.

Creative and artistic channels require tailored monetization strategies due to their unique audience demographics and engagement patterns. Unlike educational or entertainment channels, where information or amusement is the primary draw, creative channels thrive on the personal connection between the creator and their audience. This connection provides an opportunity for monetization strategies that

Monetized

are more personal and community-oriented, such as selling original artwork, offering subscription boxes, or developing apps that resonate with the audience's interests.

This chapter will explore various innovative and effective strategies for monetizing creative and artistic content. From leveraging digital marketplaces for art sales to creating immersive experiences through apps and destination centers, we will provide insights and actionable steps for creators to monetize their artistry while maintaining their creative integrity and deepening audience relationships.

PHOTOGRAPHY AND ART

Art and photography hold immense value as cultural expressions and commercial ventures. The creation process can be compelling content, offering audiences a glimpse into the artist's world, techniques, and inspirations. This process can be documented and shared through various media, providing rich content that engages and educates viewers while building a deeper connection between the artist and their audience. The following sections will explore multiple strategies for monetizing art and photography, focusing on digital marketplaces, limited editions, online galleries, collaborations, art commissions, and partnerships with physical galleries.

Digital Artwork Marketplaces

Digital platforms such as Etsy, DeviantArt, or Society6 cater to a diverse global audience, providing significant opportunities for artists to showcase and sell unique art pieces. Services like Wirestock offer the convenience of distributing to multiple platforms simultaneously. Success on these platforms hinges on optimizing listings with relevant keywords and high-quality images, regularly updating inventory, and actively engaging with the platform's community. Social media can also be a powerful tool for traffic to marketplace listings.

Artists can start by selecting a few key pieces on multiple platforms. Focus efforts on those that perform the best and engage with buyers through comments and reviews to build a loyal customer base.

Limited Editions

Limited edition prints or artworks are uniquely appealing due to their exclusivity and collectability, often justifying a higher price point.

Monetized

Artists should determine a specific number for the edition run and adhere strictly to it. Providing certificates of authenticity adds further value to these limited pieces. Introducing limited editions as special releases, possibly coinciding with significant events or milestones, and promoting them through social media can create anticipation and urgency.

Online Galleries

Creating an online gallery offers artists complete control over their presentation and branding, leading to a more personalized shopping experience for buyers. This approach requires designing an intuitive and visually appealing website, including detailed descriptions and stories behind each artwork, and implementing SEO strategies to improve online visibility. Artists like Banksy showcase their portfolios through dedicated websites, sell art, and narrate compelling stories behind each piece.

Artists can use website builders like Squarespace or WordPress, ensuring they regularly update the site with new works and engaging content.

Collaborations

Collaborating with other artists or brands opens new avenues for audience engagement and creates unique, cross-promotional opportunities. The strategy involves identifying potential collaborators whose audience aligns with the artist's style or message, co-creating artworks or products that blend both styles or brand identities, and sharing the collaborative process online to engage audiences from both sides. Artists like KAWS, known for their collaborations with brands like Nike and Uniqlo, demonstrate the potential of reaching beyond traditional art audiences.

Art Commissions

Art commissions offer a direct way for artists to connect with their audience, creating personalized artwork with special meaning for the buyer. Key strategies include publicizing commission availability through social media, setting clear commission guidelines, pricing, and timelines, and showcasing completed commissions to attract new clients. Artists like Alice X. Zhang, who share their commissioned works on social media, demonstrate the potential for gaining popularity and a steady income stream through personalized commissions.

Implementing this approach involves creating a dedicated section on the artist's website for commission inquiries and using their social media channels to periodically announce commission slots, highlighting past commissioned works to entice potential clients.

Partnerships with Physical Galleries

Partnering with physical galleries offers several significant benefits for artists, starting with enhanced visibility. Exhibiting in physical galleries increases an artist's exposure to a broader audience, including collectors and art enthusiasts who may not engage with digital platforms. This expanded reach can lead to new opportunities and connections that might not be accessible online.

Another advantage of in-person exhibitions is the opportunity for direct engagement. These events allow artists to interact personally with their audience, fostering meaningful connections and providing a platform to explain the context and inspiration behind their work. This direct interaction can deepen viewers' appreciation and understanding of the art, potentially leading to stronger emotional connections and increased sales.

Physical galleries also provide a professional presentation that can significantly enhance the perceived value of the artwork. A gallery's curated, high-quality setting can elevate the artist's work, making it more appealing to potential buyers and contributing to a more substantial reputation in the art community. The professional environment of a gallery often lends credibility and prestige, which can be pivotal in building an artist's brand.

Artists should start with thorough research and outreach to establish successful gallery partnerships. Identifying galleries that align with

Monetized

their artistic style is crucial. Once suitable galleries are identified, artists should reach out with a professional portfolio and proposal. Highlighting achievements, creative style, and how the work fits within the gallery's existing offerings can make a compelling case for collaboration.

Collaborative events are another effective strategy for maximizing the benefits of gallery partnerships. Artists can work with galleries to host events such as opening receptions, artist talks, and workshops. These events draw in new audiences and provide additional avenues for engagement, allowing artists to showcase their personality and artistic vision in a live setting.

Maintaining consistent communication with gallery partners is essential for a successful partnership. Regular discussions about exhibition schedules, promotional strategies, and feedback on displayed works ensure that both parties are aligned and can effectively promote the artist's work. This ongoing dialogue helps build a robust and collaborative relationship that can lead to long-term success.

DIGITAL PRODUCTS

Digital product sales align seamlessly with the digital nature of content creators and their audiences. By offering digital products such as graphic novels, coloring books, templates, interactive e-books, and educational content, creators can monetize their expertise and artistic talents effectively.

Modern consumers are increasingly gravitating towards digital content, favoring formats that are both accessible and engaging. Digital products, such as e-books, online courses, and digital downloads, cater to this trend by offering a seamless and convenient experience. By aligning your offerings with these preferences, you position your business to meet the demands of today's market, ensuring relevance and appeal.

Digital products immediately connect with your audience, facilitating instant access and gratification. This immediacy enhances user satisfaction and encourages repeat engagement, as consumers appreciate the ease with which they can access valuable content.

One of the most compelling advantages of digital products is their low overhead. Unlike physical products, which require significant investment in materials, manufacturing, and logistics, digital products can be produced with minimal ongoing costs. Once created, they can be replicated and sold indefinitely without needing inventory management or shipping logistics.

This inherent scalability allows creators to expand their businesses rapidly. You can distribute your digital products to a global audience without the limitations of physical boundaries. This scalability is particularly advantageous for small businesses and independent creators, enabling them to compete with larger entities on a more level playing field.

Monetized

Digital products offer a unique opportunity to gather valuable audience data. You can build a robust customer information database by offering products in exchange for email subscriptions or social media follows. This data is invaluable for future marketing campaigns, enabling you to tailor your messaging and offerings to meet your audience's needs better.

Additionally, the data collected can inform your product development process. By analyzing customer preferences and behaviors, you can identify trends and gaps in the market, allowing you to create products that are more likely to succeed. This feedback loop drives product innovation and audience growth, ensuring your business remains dynamic and responsive.

Digital products are ideal for cross-promotional strategies. For example, a tutorial video can quickly promote a related e-book, or a webinar can highlight an upcoming online course. This synergy between different types of content and products enhances the value proposition for your audience and can lead to increased sales.

Cross-promotion also maximizes the reach of your marketing efforts. By integrating your promotional activities across multiple platforms and product types, you can create a cohesive brand experience that reinforces your messaging and encourages customer loyalty.

Creating digital products that resonate with your audience can significantly enhance community building. Customers who find value in your offerings are more likely to engage with your brand and participate in community activities through online forums, social media groups, or live events.

This sense of community fosters loyalty and can lead to higher engagement rates and repeat purchases. Engaged communities are more likely to provide valuable feedback and advocate for your brand, further amplifying your reach and influence.

The sale of digital products is a logical extension for content creators. It capitalizes on the digital nature of its platform, aligns with current consumer trends, and provides a sustainable and scalable business model that enhances audience engagement and brand loyalty.

Graphic Novels

Graphic novels represent a compelling avenue for content creators to harness their storytelling and artistic skills. The strategy involves creating engaging digital graphic novels that resonate with the audience's interests and preferences. Implementation of this strategy requires using digital drawing tools to craft the novel, followed by distribution on platforms like Amazon Kindle, ComiXology, or even a personal website dedicated to the creator's work. A relevant case study is the success of webcomics like 'The Oatmeal,' which demonstrates the potential of digital platforms to boost the popularity and reach of graphic novels significantly. In the real world, platforms like Webtoon stand out as they provide a space for creators to publish and monetize their graphic novels, offering a practical route to both exposure and revenue.

Coloring Books

Coloring books, especially those themed around specific channel content, offer a unique strategy to appeal to niche audiences. Creating digital coloring books involves designing themed illustrations and compiling them into an easily downloadable PDF format. This approach has gained traction, as evidenced by the popularity of adult coloring books, signaling a broad market interest that extends beyond children. This trend underscores the potential of coloring books as a versatile product appealing to a wide age range and variety of interests.

Templates

Templates related to a channel's content—such as design layouts, photography presets, or building plans—provide another strategic opportunity for content creators. The key to this approach is creating customizable templates that meet the specific needs and preferences of the audience. Implementation involves software like Adobe Photoshop to develop and distribute these templates through the

Monetized

creator's website or online marketplaces like Etsy. A notable case study in this realm is Canva. It has revolutionized the template market with its user-friendly design options, demonstrating the high demand and potential success of well-crafted templates.

Interactive E-books

Interactive e-books present an innovative strategy, especially when they incorporate multimedia elements like videos, audio clips, or interactive quizzes. These features enrich the reading experience, making it more engaging and educational. To implement this, creators can use e-book creation tools such as Adobe InDesign and enhance their e-books with multimedia content hosted on their channel or website. A real-world example of this strategy's success can be seen in interactive cookbooks, which have gained popularity on culinary channels by providing step-by-step video guides alongside traditional recipes.

Educational Content

Producing introductory how-to guides or tutorials in a digital format capitalizes on a creator's expertise and serves as an advertisement for more comprehensive products or courses. This strategy involves writing detailed guides complemented by video or image content from the creator's channel. Such content can effectively introduce viewers to a subject, enticing them to explore more in-depth offerings. Websites like Udemy and Coursera exemplify the demand for niche educational content, providing a model for how YouTube creators can package their knowledge. An excellent real-world application of this strategy is seen in fitness influencers who release digital workout guides, combining written routines with demonstration videos, thus providing comprehensive, easy-to-follow fitness programs.

SUBSCRIPTION BOXES

Subscription boxes capitalize on the ongoing relationship between creators and their audience, offering a tangible, personalized experience beyond the digital realm. For content creators, subscription boxes represent an opportunity to deepen audience engagement, diversify revenue streams, and enhance their brand's value through physical products and exclusive content.

The rationale behind adopting subscription boxes is their ability to create a community-centric experience. In a digital world where content is often consumed passively, receiving a curated box transforms the viewer's interaction with the creator into a more active and personal engagement. This model fosters loyalty and taps into the audience's desire for exclusive, tangible connections with their favorite creators.

Furthermore, for content creators, subscription boxes are a practical extension of their digital presence, allowing them to leverage their existing audience successfully. Creators can utilize their understanding of their viewers' preferences and interests to tailor the contents of the boxes, ensuring relevance and appeal. This direct line to a dedicated audience base reduces marketing costs and increases the likelihood of sustained subscription renewals.

Additionally, subscription boxes offer a unique avenue for brand collaborations and partnerships, broadening the scope of content and introducing new products to an engaged audience. This enhances the value of each box and opens up additional revenue channels for creators through partnerships and sponsorships.

Monetized

Themed Boxes

Subscription boxes offer a unique and tangible connection between content creators and their audience, especially pertinent in creative and artistic channels. For instance, a drawing channel curating themed boxes with art supplies directly caters to its audience's interests and needs. This approach satisfies the viewers' desire for related products and enhances engagement by integrating these supplies into the channel's content.

The key to success in themed boxes is in their curation. Creators should consider assembling a monthly or quarterly box with unique art supplies, perhaps even aligning with specific techniques or styles featured on the channel. To add more value, including an exclusive piece of art or a tutorial utilizing the items in the box can make the package more appealing and instructional.

'SketchBox' and 'ArtSnacks' demonstrate the effectiveness of this approach. These platforms offer monthly subscriptions that provide premium art supplies and unique artistic challenges, aligning perfectly with their target audience's interests and needs.

Exclusive Content

Incorporating exclusive content into subscription boxes adds a layer of exclusivity and privilege, which can be a significant draw for potential subscribers. Exclusive items could range from signed prints and behind-the-scenes videos to early access to content, offering subscribers something special that isn't available to the general audience.

Developing digital content such as tutorials, e-books, or online workshops that complement the physical items in the box is crucial. This exclusive digital content should be accessible only to the subscribers, adding a sense of exclusivity and value to the subscription.

'Loot Crate' exemplifies this approach by offering exclusive collectibles and apparel in their themed boxes. These items are often

Monetized

not available for purchase elsewhere, adding to the allure of the subscription.

Collaborations with Brands

Collaborating with relevant brands can significantly enhance the value of a subscription box. This strategy includes quality products in the boxes and diversifies the contents, making each box more appealing and valuable.

Content creators should aim to identify and partner with brands aligning with their channel's content and audience's interests. These could be art supply manufacturers, local artisan shops, or even tech companies offering digital art tools. Such partnerships can provide diverse and high-quality products for the boxes.

'FabFitFun' is a notable example in this regard. The company collaborates with various lifestyle brands to include a mix of beauty, wellness, and home products in their subscription boxes, catering to a broad audience base.

Community Feedback

Utilizing subscriber feedback is essential in ensuring that the subscription boxes remain relevant, desirable, and community-driven. This approach allows creators to tailor their boxes according to the preferences and suggestions of their subscribers, fostering a sense of community and ensuring subscriber satisfaction.

Regularly conducting survey polls or establishing a dedicated feedback section on the website or social media platforms is a practical approach. This feedback should be used to directly influence the curation of future boxes, ensuring that they align with subscriber preferences and expectations.

'Birchbox' effectively utilizes this strategy. The company actively encourages subscribers to rate and review the products they receive. This feedback is then used to customize future boxes, making each one more tailored to the preferences of their subscriber base.

Monetized

APP DEVELOPMENT

App development is a flexible platform for audience engagement and revenue generation. The rationale behind this approach lies in the direct connection creators have with their audience, providing insights into their preferences, needs, and behaviors.

Firstly, content creators often profoundly understand their audience's interests and challenges, gained through interactions in comments, live streams, and social media engagement. This knowledge is invaluable in developing app concepts that resonate with their target audience. For instance, a cooking channel creator might recognize their audience's need for an interactive recipe app, or a fitness vlogger might see the demand for a personalized workout app.

Moreover, the trust and rapport built with viewers over time translate into a ready and receptive market for new products. Fans of a YouTube channel are more likely to show interest in and support for apps that extend the content they already enjoy. This established audience can be an initial user base for the app, providing early feedback and promoting organic growth through word-of-mouth.

In addition, content creators can use their platforms to market their apps effectively. Regular exposure in videos, mentions in descriptions, and demonstrations of the app's features can drive downloads and engagement. This integrated marketing strategy is cost-effective and can reach a broad audience rapidly.

When brainstorming app ideas, creators should start by identifying gaps or unmet needs in their niche. Analyzing audience feedback, conducting surveys, and monitoring trends can offer insights into what kind of app would add value to their viewers' experience. It's also crucial to consider the unique aspects of their content that can be translated into an app. For example, an art channel might develop an

Monetized app that allows users to follow along with tutorials using interactive tools.

In summary, app development as a business model for influencers makes sense due to the direct access to and understanding of their audience. This model provides a new avenue for monetization and deepens audience engagement, leveraging the creator's brand and content in a dynamic digital marketplace.

Complementary Apps

Complementary apps naturally extend a channel's content, supplementing the client experience with interactive and valuable tools. These apps can provide additional value by offering practical applications of the content shared on YouTube. For instance, an art channel can significantly benefit from a painting tutorial app that includes step-by-step guides, color mixing techniques, and virtual workshops.

The success of apps like Bob Ross's 'The Joy of Painting,' which offers an immersive experience through tutorials and a virtual canvas for practice, showcases the effectiveness of this strategy. Adobe's suite of apps also demonstrates how tools can complement and extend the value of creative YouTube tutorials, providing an integrated learning experience for users.

Developing such apps requires a deep understanding of the audience's needs. The app should feature a user-friendly interface and functionalities that directly relate to and enrich the existing content. For example, offering direct access to premium video tutorials within the app can streamline the user experience.

Educational Apps

Educational apps align perfectly with channels focused on teaching and learning. These apps can offer structured and engaging learning experiences, whether about budgeting and financial planning, as seen in Dave Ramsey's EveryDollar app, or other educational subjects.

Monetized

Apps like Duolingo, which supplements language learning channels with interactive lessons, exemplify how educational apps can effectively extend existing content.

The key to a successful educational app lies in creating content that is both engaging and easy to digest. Incorporating gamification elements can significantly enhance user engagement and retention. Regular updates and the addition of new content are also crucial for maintaining the app's relevance and appeal.

Khan Academy's app extends its educational YouTube content into structured courses, quizzes, and progress-tracking features, demonstrating how an app can effectively complement and expand upon a channel's academic content.

Interactive Experiences

Interactive apps engage the audience at a deeper level compared to passive video content. Through gamification, they can turn learning and engagement into a more enjoyable and memorable experience.

For example, an art channel might develop a drawing game that challenges users to recreate art pieces featured in videos. Music channels can create apps that allow users to compose music with virtual instruments, adding an interactive dimension to their learning experience.

Effective interactive apps should feature engaging UI/UX designs and gamification techniques such as rewards, challenges, and leaderboards. Accessibility for various skill levels is essential to cater to a broad audience.

Headspace's meditation app, which offers interactive sessions complementing its YouTube mindfulness content, is a prime example. The app uses engaging graphics and progress tracking to enhance the user experience.

Monetized

Monetization Models

App monetization presents a significant opportunity for revenue generation, with in-app purchases and subscriptions serving as continuous income streams. This approach is especially relevant in today's app market, where ongoing user engagement is crucial.

Freemium models, where the app is free but certain features require payment, can effectively attract many potential users. Offering subscriptions for premium content creates a steady flow of income. However, the conversion rate from free to paid users is notoriously low. This could mean access to additional courses or exclusive materials for educational apps.

The balance between free and premium features is critical. Free features should offer genuine value, while premium features need to provide significant additional benefits. Regularly updating the app with new features and content can encourage ongoing subscriptions and user engagement.

The Calm app employs a tiered subscription model, offering essential content for free while reserving advanced features and exclusive content for paid subscribers. This approach demonstrates how well-implemented monetization models can attract and retain users, contributing to the app's overall success.

DESTINATION CENTERS

The evolution of digital content creation has opened avenues for creators to engage with their audience beyond the virtual space. The Destination Center model represents this shift, offering a tangible, interactive experience that extends the creator's brand into the physical world. This business model is particularly viable for content creators due to several key factors.

Firstly, the pre-existing audience base of a successful channel is a valuable asset. These followers are often highly engaged and invested in the creator's content, making them a ready market for additional experiences and products offered at a Destination Center. This audience loyalty translates into a reliable customer base, reducing the initial risk typically associated with new ventures.

Secondly, content creators are uniquely positioned to deeply understand their audience's preferences and interests. This insight allows them to tailor the offerings of their Destination Center to meet specific needs and desires, whether it's selling niche products, hosting specialized workshops, or creating events that resonate with their community.

Moreover, integrating a physical space with a digital presence creates a synergy that enhances both. The Destination Center provides content for the digital channel, such as live events or workshops, while the digital channel drives traffic to the physical location. This interplay boosts engagement across both platforms and opens up diverse revenue streams.

Opening up a content creation studio to visitors can be a significant draw and asset for a brick-and-mortar establishment. By inviting the public into the creative process, the studio can offer a unique, behind-the-scenes experience that not only demystifies the art of content creation but also fosters a deeper connection with the audience. Visitors can witness firsthand the intricate work of producing high-quality content, from filming and editing to graphic design and sound engineering. This transparency can build trust and loyalty among fans, making them feel more invested in the brand.

In addition, the Destination Center model capitalizes on the trend of experiential retail and interactive experiences. Modern consumers, particularly those who follow creative and artistic channels, increasingly seek experiences they can participate in and share rather than just products to purchase. This shift in consumer behavior aligns perfectly with the interactive and community-focused nature of Destination Centers. Hosting tours, workshops, and interactive sessions generate additional revenue streams and attract a diverse clientele, from aspiring creators seeking inspiration and education to tourists looking for unique local experiences.

Furthermore, allowing customers to take pictures in an iconic studio setting would be a significant grassroots marketing opportunity. These photos, shared on social media, serve as authentic endorsements, spreading word-of-mouth about the studio and creating organic buzz. Such engagement can enhance the studio's reputation and visibility, driving foot traffic to the physical location and ultimately bolstering the establishment's overall success and community presence.

Finally, this model offers a sustainable way for content creators to diversify their income. Rather than relying solely on online ad revenue or sponsorships, a Destination Center provides a more stable and controllable income source. It also offers the flexibility to adapt and expand offerings based on changing trends and audience feedback, ensuring long-term relevance and profitability.

In conclusion, the Destination Center business model makes sense for content creators because it leverages their existing audience, provides opportunities for diversified revenue, and aligns with current consumer preferences for interactive and experiential engagement. By bridging the gap between the digital and physical realms, content creators can create a unique space that embodies their brand and offers a new way to connect with and monetize their audience.

Storefront for Niche Gear

Leveraging a content creator's influence to establish a storefront for niche gear can be a highly effective strategy. By aligning the products with the channel's theme, creators can capitalize on their audience's interests. For example, an art-focused channel could successfully sell high-quality art supplies, exclusive merchandise, or custom creations. This approach resembles a channel like 'Proko,' known for its instructional art videos, opening a retail space offering sketchbooks, drawing tools, and anatomical models. Implementing this idea involves selecting a location with substantial foot traffic, sourcing products in high demand among the audience, and integrating an e-commerce platform for online sales. The channel is a powerful marketing tool, promoting the storefront and offering exclusive deals to subscribers.

Content Generation Participation

Encouraging audience participation in content generation is a strategy that can significantly deepen viewer engagement and provide fresh content for the channel. This approach involves actively inviting subscribers to partake in the content creation process. For instance, a cooking channel might invite its audience to participate in cooking sessions filmed in a professional kitchen setup. To implement this, designated areas within the center should be prepared for filming. Regular content creation events should be scheduled and promoted through social media and the channel. It is also crucial to ensure that all legal and safety protocols are in place for public participation.

Workshops and Classes

Hosting educational sessions such as workshops and classes aligns perfectly with the content of many channels, offering value-added experiences to the audience. A photography channel, for example, could conduct weekend studio photography workshops to teach skills

Monetized

like portrait photography or Photoshop editing. Implementing this strategy involves developing a detailed curriculum, employing skilled instructors or leading the sessions personally, and advertising these workshops through the channel. Offering in-person and virtual options can help reach a broader audience, catering to local and remote followers.

Event Hosting

Utilizing the Destination Center for hosting events like meet-and-greets, product launches, or exhibitions is an effective strategy to foster community and brand loyalty. A gaming channel, for instance, could organize game release parties or eSports tournaments, thereby creating a communal space for the gaming audience. To implement this, it's important to plan events that resonate with the channel's theme, create a well-structured event schedule, and promote them to the audience through various digital platforms. Collaborating with brands for sponsorships or featuring specific products can add value to these events.

MiniWarGaming's Bunker

MiniWarGaming provides a notable example of successfully implementing the Destination Center model. They transformed their space into a multi-functional hub for fans of miniature wargaming, featuring gaming areas, thematic video production studios, a store selling miniatures and gear, and facilities for overnight stays. Their multifaceted approach includes hosting gaming events and tournaments, offering memberships for exclusive access, selling branded merchandise, and filming battles and tutorials in custom-built sets. This strategy generates revenue and cements its position as a central hub in its community, highlighting the potential of a Destination Center to enhance brand presence and profitability.

Monetized

LIFESTYLE CONTENT AND PERSONAL VLOGS

Lifestyle and Personal Vlog channels, characterized by their focus on day-to-day experiences, personal interests, and direct engagement with viewers, have carved out a significant niche in the digital content landscape. This chapter delves into the monetization strategies specifically suited for creators in this genre, underlining why these methods differ fundamentally from those applicable to other types of content.

YouTube and Twitch's lifestyle and personal vlogging sectors have witnessed exponential growth. This surge can be attributed to the authentic and relatable nature of the content, which resonates deeply with audiences seeking genuine connections and real-life experiences. The market analysis reveals that subscribers of these channels often form a loyal and engaged community drawn to the creators' personal stories, life tips, and experiential insights. This high level of engagement presents unique monetization opportunities distinct from more informational or entertainment-focused channels.

Unlike channels centered on education, gaming, or specific hobbies, lifestyle and personal vlog channels thrive on the personality and life experiences of the creator. These channels often blend various elements - from travel and fashion to family life and personal wellness - creating a rich tapestry of content that appeals to a diverse audience. This personal touch transforms viewers into a community, making the content more than just a source of entertainment or information but a part of their daily lives.

The marketing strategies for these channels are inherently different. They rely heavily on personal branding, community engagement, and authenticity. The audience's trust and connection with the creator are pivotal, making transparent and genuine marketing approaches more effective. This relationship-driven approach demands unique monetization strategies that capitalize on audience size, quality, and engagement levels.

Monetized

The monetization strategies in this realm extend beyond traditional advertising revenues. They encompass a range of activities, from exclusive events and personalized products to life coaching and freelance writing. Each strategy leverages the personal connection between the creator and their audience, turning every interaction into an opportunity for deeper engagement and monetization.

We will explore these strategies in detail as we delve deeper into this chapter. We will provide insights into how lifestyle and personal vlog content creators can effectively monetize their unique position in the digital content ecosystem. This chapter uses market analysis, practical tips, and real-world examples to equip creators with the tools and knowledge to transform their passion into a sustainable and profitable venture.

MEET AND GREETS

Meet and greets are a pivotal business model for lifestyle and personal vlog content creators, primarily due to their ability to forge a deeper, more personal connection with the audience. This model is rooted in the fundamental principle of personal branding, where the creator's personality and life experiences become the centerpiece of their content. The audience engages with the content and the creator in such a scenario. This unique dynamic offers a powerful platform for monetization through direct interactions.

The Value of Personal Connection

The justification for incorporating meet and greets into a content creator's business strategy lies in their inherent nature of personalization and community building. These events transcend the conventional creator-viewer relationship, fostering the audience's sense of belonging and loyalty. This loyalty is crucial, as it enhances the viewers' engagement with the channel and increases their willingness to participate in paid events and offerings.

Moreover, the craving for real human connections is more pronounced in an increasingly digital world. Meet and greets satisfy this craving, offering a tangible experience that deepens the audience's connection to the creator. This creates a unique opportunity for the content creator to leverage their brand, transforming viewers into a dedicated community. This community not only supports the creator through direct participation in events but also serves as a vital asset for word-of-mouth marketing and brand expansion.

The diversity in the meet-and-greet format– from online to in-person to hybrid models – allows creators to tap into different audience segments. Online events cater to a global audience, breaking geographical barriers and offering inclusivity, while in-person events

Monetized

provide an irreplaceable personal touch that strengthens community bonds. The hybrid model maximizes reach and engagement, appealing to local and international audiences.

In summary, meet and greets as a business model make sense for lifestyle and personal vlog content creators due to their ability to capitalize on the personal connection with the audience. This strategy enhances audience loyalty and engagement and opens up diverse revenue streams, making it a practical and effective approach to monetization in the digital content landscape.

Online Meet and Greets

Online meet and greets harness the power of digital platforms like Zoom, Google Meet, or specialized event platforms to bridge the gap between content creators and their global audience. The key to success in these virtual events is incorporating interactive elements that keep the audience engaged. This can include live Q&A sessions, allowing for real-time interaction, virtual photo opportunities that mimic the experience of an in-person event, and live performances or demonstrations that add a unique and personal touch. These interactive elements enhance the audience's understanding and elevate the event's perceived value, making it more memorable and engaging.

In-Person Meet and Greets

In-person meet and greets are organized with a focus on accessibility and comfort, ensuring that the venues chosen are easily reachable and secure for both the creator and the attendees. These events often include activities like autograph signings, photo sessions, and the sale of merchandise, which serve as an additional revenue stream and as tangible memories for the attendees. The intimate nature of these events fosters a stronger connection between the creator and their audience, creating a loyal fan base that is more likely to engage with future content and events.

A practical example can be observed in a beauty vlogger who collaborates with a makeup brand to host a meet and greet at a retail location. This collaboration brings the vlogger's online persona into a physical space and allows live demonstrations and makeovers. The hands-on experience with the products and the personal interaction with the vlogger create a unique and immersive experience for attendees, enhancing brand loyalty and audience engagement.

Hybrid Events

Hybrid events blend the reach of online streaming with the intimacy of in-person events. A practical implementation of this model can be seen in the strategy adopted by musician and YouTuber Lindsey Stirling, who hosts concerts with both a live audience and an online stream. This approach allows for a broader reach, engaging both local attendees and an international online audience. The key to a successful hybrid event is seamlessly integrating the in-person and online experiences, ensuring both audiences feel equally valued and involved.

VIP Experiences

VIP experiences elevate the standard meet-and-greet format by offering premium options such as private dinners, backstage access, or personalized gifts. These exclusive experiences cater to a segment of the audience willing to pay a premium for a more intimate interaction with the creator. A real-world example of this model is lifestyle influencer Mr. Kate, who offers VIP tickets for interior design workshops, including personal consultations. Such experiences not only generate additional revenue but also deepen the fan-creator relationship.

Collaborative Events

Collaborative events involve partnering with other creators or brands to host joint events, expanding the potential audience, and pooling resources for a more significant impact. For instance, Tech YouTubers Marques Brownlee and Unbox Therapy co-host a tech expo showcasing the latest gadgets and hosting discussions. These collaborations bring together diverse audiences, increase the event's reach and appeal, and provide a platform for cross-promotion among the collaborating parties.

Conventions and Trade Shows

Conventions and trade shows offer a significant opportunity for content creators to engage with many potential customers within their niche. These events gather enthusiasts, industry professionals, and influencers in one place, creating a fertile ground for networking, brand exposure, and direct audience interaction. For content creators, participating in conventions and trade shows can lead to new partnerships, sponsorships, and an expanded fan base. The concentrated environment of these events allows creators to showcase their work, engage with their audience in real-time, and establish a more substantial presence within their industry.

Effective Planning and Logistics

Effective planning and logistics are crucial, particularly when considering the venue, timing, audience demographics, and technical needs. Marketing and promotion play a significant role, utilizing channels like social media, email newsletters, and YouTube videos to reach potential attendees. Interactive segments, both in online and in-person formats, are vital in maintaining audience engagement. After the event, engagement continues through follow-up communications, feedback surveys, and the sharing of highlight reels. Monetization strategies vary, encompassing ticket sales, merchandise, sponsored content, and exclusive post-event content. In online settings, options like pay-per-view or exclusive access to recorded content can be effective.

Local Meetups

Local meetups cultivate community, enabling viewers to connect directly with the creator. These gatherings are instrumental in building a loyal fan base and providing a platform for direct feedback and interaction. Local meetups strengthen the bond between content creators and their audience by creating a more

Monetized

intimate and personal setting, fostering a supportive and engaged community.

Venue Selection

Choosing the right venue is critical to the success of a local meetup. Opt for central and accessible locations that cater to the convenience of most of the audience. Venues should be easily reachable by public transportation and offer adequate parking facilities. Consider factors such as seating capacity, audio-visual equipment, and ambiance to ensure a comfortable and engaging experience for attendees.

Event Format

The format of the local meetup should reflect the channel's style and the audience's preferences. Options range from informal gatherings, where attendees can socialize and network freely, to structured Q&A sessions that provide a platform for direct interaction and discussion. Networking events can also be influential, allowing attendees to connect with the creator in a more formal setting.

For instance, tech influencers often leverage local meetups, particularly at tech conferences or expos, to engage with their audience. These events offer a platform for direct interaction and networking, allowing creators to showcase new products, answer questions, and gather valuable feedback from their audience.

Local Partnerships

Collaborating with local businesses can enhance the accessibility and appeal of the event. Partnering with local venues for space arrangements or securing sponsorships can reduce costs and provide additional resources for the event. These partnerships can also offer mutual promotional opportunities, increasing visibility for both the creator and the local businesses involved.

Monetized

Community Involvement

Involving the community in planning ensures that the event aligns with their interests and expectations. Actively seek feedback from your audience through surveys, social media polls, or direct communication to understand their preferences and needs. Encouraging community involvement enhances the event's relevance and fosters a sense of ownership and engagement among attendees.

Safety Considerations

Safety is paramount when organizing meet-and-greet events, whether they are in-person or online. Ensuring the security and well-being of both the creator and the attendees is essential, particularly given the dynamics of parasocial behavior—a phenomenon where fans develop one-sided relationships with public figures, feeling a deep connection despite little or no interaction. While these relationships can foster positive engagement and loyalty, they can also lead to unrealistic expectations or inappropriate behavior from some fans, which needs careful management.

In-Person Events

For in-person events, the choice of venue plays a critical role in ensuring safety. Venues must have adequate security measures, such as trained security personnel, secure entry points, and clear emergency protocols. Adherence to health and safety regulations, including provisions for crowd control, is essential to manage large gatherings and prevent incidents.

Security Personnel

Employing trained security staff to monitor the event can help manage any issues that arise swiftly and efficiently. Security personnel should be briefed on the specific dynamics of fan interactions to be vigilant about potential problems stemming from parasocial behavior.

Monetized

Secure Entry Points

Controlled entry and exit points ensure only authorized individuals can access the event. This reduces the risk of unauthorized persons disrupting the event and helps maintain an orderly flow of attendees.

Emergency Protocols

Establishing clear procedures for handling emergencies, including medical issues and security threats, is crucial. These protocols should be well-communicated to all staff and volunteers.

Crowd Control

Effective crowd control measures, such as barriers, clear signage, and designated areas, help manage the flow of attendees and prevent overcrowding. This not only ensures safety but also enhances the overall experience for attendees.

Online Events

For online meet and greets, digital security is of utmost importance. Utilizing secure platforms, protecting attendee data, and ensuring safe online interactions are essential to building trust and safeguarding the community.

Secure Platforms

Choosing reputable platforms with robust security features like encryption and two-factor authentication helps protect against unauthorized access and data breaches.

Monetized

Data Protection

Ensuring attendee information is securely stored and not shared without consent is critical for maintaining privacy and trust.

Moderation Tools

Implementing moderation tools allows for monitoring and managing interactions during the event. This includes the ability to remove inappropriate content or behavior quickly.

Guidelines for Conduct

Establishing and communicating rules for participant behavior helps maintain a respectful and safe environment. These guidelines should be visible and enforced consistently to deter any potential disruptions.

Addressing Parasocial Behavior

Parasocial relationships, while often a natural and harmless part of being a fan, can sometimes escalate into unhealthy or disruptive behavior. Creators and organizers must be vigilant and prepared to address such issues effectively to ensure the safety and well-being of both the creator and their audience. Understanding and managing parasocial behavior involves recognizing potential problems, setting clear boundaries, providing appropriate support, and fostering healthy interactions.

Recognizing Red Flags

Being alert to signs of unhealthy attachment is crucial. Parasocial behavior can manifest in various ways, such as obsessive messaging, unrealistic expectations, or attempts to breach the creator's privacy. Fans may exhibit an intense need for attention or validation from the creator, believing they have a special connection. This can lead to persistent attempts to contact the creator through multiple channels, unsolicited gifts, or showing up unannounced at public appearances.

Creators and their teams should be trained to recognize these red flags. Monitoring fan interactions on social media and during live events can help identify individuals displaying concerning behavior. Early detection allows for timely intervention, preventing potential issues from escalating.

Setting Clear Boundaries

Establishing and communicating clear boundaries is essential for managing parasocial behavior. Creators should articulate what types of interactions are appropriate and which are not. This includes limiting direct messages, personal questions, and physical interactions at meet and greets.

For instance, creators can make it known that while they appreciate fan engagement, they cannot personally respond to every message or comment. During in-person events, boundaries regarding physical contact and the duration of interactions should be clearly stated and enforced. Consistently applying these boundaries helps fans understand and respect the creator's personal space and limits.

Providing Support

It is beneficial to offer resources and support for fans who may need help managing their feelings. Many fans form parasocial relationships as a way to cope with personal challenges or loneliness. Providing access to mental health resources, such as counseling services or hotlines, can be a valuable way to support these individuals.

Creators can also collaborate with mental health professionals to develop educational content that addresses the nature of parasocial relationships and promotes healthy coping strategies. By showing empathy and understanding, creators can help fans constructively navigate their emotions.

Encouraging Healthy Interaction

Promoting healthy fan engagement is vital for maintaining a positive community atmosphere. Creators should encourage respectful communication and model appropriate behavior in their interactions. This involves responding to fans in a kind but professional way, avoiding over-familiarity that could blur the lines of the relationship.

Engagement activities that emphasize community rather than personal connection can also help. For example, creators can organize group activities such as Q&A sessions, live streams, and fan art showcases that allow fans to interact with each other and the creator in a controlled and respectful environment.

Implementing Security Measures

In addition to setting boundaries and providing support, practical security measures should be in place to protect both the creator and their fans. This includes:

- **Privacy Controls**: Adjusting privacy settings on social media to limit direct access to the creator.
- **Moderation Tools**: Utilizing moderation tools during online events to quickly address inappropriate behavior.
- **Emergency Contacts**: Plan to contact authorities if a situation escalates beyond what can be managed internally.

Open Communication

Maintaining open lines of communication with the fan community is essential. Creators should regularly update their audience on their boundaries and expectations. This can be done through social media posts, videos, and live interactions. Transparency about the reasons behind these boundaries helps fans understand and accept them.

Monetized

By addressing parasocial behavior comprehensively, creators can create a safer and more enjoyable environment for everyone involved. This proactive approach protects the creator's well-being and promotes a healthy, respectful, and engaged community. Through vigilance, clear communication, and supportive resources, the potential negative impacts of parasocial relationships can be effectively managed, allowing for positive and enriching interactions between creators and their fans.

PHYSICAL PRODUCTS

By translating the tangible elements of their brand into physical products, creators add a new dimension to their product offering, deepening audience involvement and loyalty at a higher margin than affiliate marketing.

For content creators, particularly those in niches like crafts, DIY, lifestyle, or beauty, the move to sell physical products aligns seamlessly with their existing content. These creators often showcase or use various products in their videos, which naturally piques the interest of their viewers. By offering these products for sale, creators respond to existing audience interest, ensuring a ready market for their goods.

Moreover, the audience of a YouTube channel is not just a group of passive viewers; they are engaged fans who often seek to emulate or draw inspiration from the content. Selling physical products allows these fans to own a piece of the content they admire. This form of merchandise symbolizes their connection to the creator and the community around the channel.

When a creator endorses a product, especially one they have had a hand in creating or curating, it carries significant weight with their audience. This trust translates into consumer confidence, making viewers more likely to purchase products directly from the creator rather than from unrelated third-party vendors.

It reduces over-reliance on traditional online monetization methods like advertising or sponsorships, which can be unpredictable. The direct-to-consumer approach in selling physical products also ensures greater control over the brand narrative and customer experience, crucial in maintaining brand integrity and audience satisfaction.

Monetized

Venturing into the realm of physical products is not just a means of revenue generation; it's a strategic move to enhance brand value, deepen audience relationships, and solidify their presence in both the digital and physical worlds.

Crafts and DIY Products

Leveraging a content creator's channel to create and sell handmade items or DIY kits is a direct approach to monetizing their creative skills and audience interest. Implementation of this strategy involves several key steps. Firstly, it requires identifying popular projects or themes that resonate with the audience. This insight can be gleaned from viewer feedback and the popularity of specific videos. Once these themes are identified, the next step is to source materials and create prototypes. These products should reflect the content and quality viewers expect from the channel.

After the products are developed, the next crucial step is choosing the right platforms for sales. Marketplaces like Etsy and Amazon Handmade are excellent for creators specializing in handmade or unique items while selling through a personal website, which allows for greater brand control. Additionally, showcasing the creation process in videos can significantly boost audience interest and engagement, turning viewers into potential customers.

A real-world example of this strategy can be seen in Black Tail Studio, which specializes in woodworking and epoxy tables. Such creators might sell finished handmade wooden furniture, epoxy kits, or DIY woodworking kits for beginners, directly linking their online content with physical products.

Limited Editions

Creating limited-edition products is a strategy that thrives on exclusivity and urgency. The implementation of this strategy starts with designing a unique, time-bound product line that is distinct and appealing to the audience. To maximize impact, these products should be promoted heavily before the launch. To build anticipation and excitement, this can be achieved through various marketing tactics such as countdowns, email marketing, and social media campaigns.

Furthermore, influencer marketing can be employed to extend the reach of these products beyond the creator's immediate audience. By collaborating with influencers with a similar target audience, creators can tap into new markets and drive additional sales.

Product Collaborations

Product collaboration strategies involve partnering with established brands to create co-branded products. This approach leverages the brand's audience and the creator's creativity. Implementing this strategy starts with identifying brands that align with the channel's values and audience. Once a suitable partner is found, the next step is to negotiate a mutually beneficial partnership.

Collaboration in product design and marketing strategies ensures that the final product resonates with both the creator's audience and the brand's customers. The product launch should be coordinated, utilizing both the creator's channel and the brand's platforms for maximum exposure.

A case study illustrates this approach with beauty vloggers who partner with cosmetic brands to create signature makeup lines. These collaborations often result in products that embody the vlogger's style and expertise, making them highly appealing to their followers.

Marketplaces for Selling Physical Products

Choosing the right marketplace is crucial for the success of physical products. Etsy and Amazon Handmade are ideal for individual creators and small businesses focusing on handmade or unique items, offering vast audiences and credibility. For creators seeking complete control over branding and customer experience, setting up an e-commerce store using platforms like Shopify or WooCommerce is a viable option. Social media platforms like Instagram and Facebook also have marketplace features that facilitate direct sales.

Monetized

For those with a significant local following, participating in pop-up shops or local markets can effectively reach customers.

Considerations

When venturing into the sale of physical products, several considerations are paramount. Quality control is critical to maintaining the brand's reputation; thus, ensuring that all products meet a high standard is essential. Providing excellent customer service enhances customer satisfaction and encourages repeat business, fostering a loyal customer base. Effective marketing and promotion through the creator's YouTube channel and other social media platforms are vital in driving sales and awareness of the products. Lastly, regularly gathering customer feedback and adapting products or strategies is crucial for continuous improvement and attention to audience preferences.

LIFE COACHING

Establishing a direct, personal connection with the audience is paramount in a successful Life Coaching endeavor. Creators who venture into life coaching are diversifying their revenue streams and deepening their engagement with their audience.

Over time, content creators become authoritative figures in their respective niches- wellness, motivation, or personal development. This authority positions them ideally for life coaching, where trust and expertise are crucial. By offering life coaching services, they can leverage their existing audience base, which already resonates with their message and is likely to seek personalized guidance.

Moreover, life coaching aligns seamlessly with the content already being produced. For instance, a YouTuber focusing on self-improvement can easily extend their online advice into more tailored, one-on-one coaching sessions. This extension feels natural to the audience, who are already familiar with the creator's style and philosophy.

Additionally, life coaching offers a scalable business model. While one-on-one sessions are time-bound, group workshops and digital resources like webinars or e-books can reach a broader audience without significantly more effort. This scalability benefits content creators, who often must balance content creation with other business endeavors.

Furthermore, life coaching as a monetization strategy addresses a growing demand for personalized, accessible guidance in various aspects of life. With the rise of digital platforms, people are increasingly seeking advice and mentorship online, a need that content creators are uniquely positioned to meet. Their role as life coaches is not just a business venture but a response to a societal shift towards digital mentorship and guidance.

Monetized

Life Coaching capitalizes on the trust and authority influencers have built, offers scalability, and meets a growing market demand for digital mentorship. It is a strategic choice for content creators looking to expand their influence and revenue streams.

Personalized Sessions

In the personalized sessions model, YouTube content creators offer individualized coaching to address the specific needs of their audience. This approach allows for tailored guidance covering diverse topics such as goal setting, personal development, and career advice. The key to successful implementation lies in efficient organization and communication. Tools like Calendly streamline scheduling, while platforms like Zoom facilitate virtual meetings. Secure payment gateways ensure smooth transactions. A prominent example in this domain is Tony Robbins, who utilizes his YouTube presence to extend his reach and offer personalized coaching. This model thrives on the direct, impactful connection between the coach and the client, making it an effective strategy for creators looking to leverage their influence in a more intimate setting.

Subscription Coaching Services

The subscription coaching model presents a sustainable and consistent revenue stream. It offers subscribers ongoing access to coaching services, including weekly group calls, Q&A sessions, or exclusive content. This model fosters a sense of community and continuous engagement. Implementation can be streamlined using platforms like Patreon or Memberful, which manage subscriptions efficiently. Marie Forleo's subscription-based business coaching program exemplifies this model's success. By providing regular, structured interactions, creators can maintain ongoing relationships with their audience, encouraging long-term engagement and loyalty.

Digital Resources

Offering digital resources such as e-books, workbooks, and exclusive video content is an effective strategy to complement life coaching services. These resources add significant value, enhancing the learning experience. They can be sold separately or used as marketing tools to attract more clients. For distribution and sales, platforms like Gumroad or Shopify are ideal. This approach diversifies the income streams and helps reach a broader audience who may prefer self-paced learning options.

Certification and Credibility

Gaining certifications from accredited coaching institutions is crucial in enhancing credibility and trustworthiness. Content creators need to showcase their qualifications and expertise, particularly in a field as personal as life coaching. Enrollment in certification programs from bodies like the International Coach Federation (ICF) can significantly bolster a creator's authority in the coaching field. Mel Robbins serves as a prime example, where her status as a certified life coach adds substantial credibility and attracts a broader clientele.

Building a Coaching Brand

Content creators venturing into life coaching must concentrate on building a robust and authentic brand. This involves creating a professional website, developing a unique coaching methodology, and consistently producing content that resonates with their coaching niche. A strong brand identity helps distinguish the company's services in a crowded market.

Marketing and Promotion

Effectively utilizing YouTube and other social media platforms for marketing and promotion is indispensable. Key strategies include sharing client testimonials, excerpts from coaching sessions, and regular content highlighting the creator's expertise. These efforts increase visibility and establish the creator's reputation as a knowledgeable and trustworthy coach.

Monetized

Engagement and Community Building

Engaging directly with the audience is crucial for building a loyal community. This can be achieved through interactive comments, live Q&A sessions, and community posts on YouTube. Offering free resources or initial consultation sessions can incentivize potential clients to explore the coaching services. This level of engagement fosters a strong connection between the creator and their audience, paving the way for a thriving coaching practice.

FREELANCE WRITING

Freelance writing for YouTube content creators is an excellent way to leverage their expertise and visibility, expanding their reach beyond their channel and establishing themselves as authorities in their field. This can be achieved through guest blogging and column writing.

Guest Blogging

Guest blogging is where content creators write and publish articles on other websites or blogs, usually in a niche similar to theirs. This strategy allows creators to tap into new audiences, enhance their search engine rankings with backlinks, and forge industry relationships. It is a platform for sharing expertise and gaining exposure, thus establishing credibility.

The power of guest blogging lies in its ability to reach diverse audiences and build a creator's profile. For instance, a technology vlogger can benefit from writing for renowned tech websites like TechCrunch or Wired, introducing their content to a broader, tech-savvy audience. The process begins with identifying suitable blogs that align with the creator's niche and possess a significant reader base. Effective pitching is critical here; pitches should be concise, personalized, and demonstrate a clear understanding of the target blog's audience. A notable example includes a travel vlogger creating a unique travel guide for Lonely Planet, showcasing their expertise to travel enthusiasts.

Quality content is vital in guest blogging. Articles should provide value, engage readers, and reflect the creator's deep understanding of the subject. The financial aspect also plays a role, as guest bloggers are often compensated per article, offering a viable source of income.

Monetized

To implement this strategy effectively, creators should first build a portfolio of writing samples, possibly through blog posts on their website. Networking is crucial; leveraging social media and professional networks to connect with blog owners and editors is essential. Regularly sending pitches to various blogs and maintaining persistence can result in successful guest blogging opportunities.

Column Writing

Column writing involves a more consistent relationship with publications, where creators regularly contribute articles to magazines or online platforms. This method provides steady exposure and can help establish the creator as a thought leader in their niche, often leading to a consistent income stream.

The primary context for column writing is to enhance visibility and establish authority. Selecting the right platforms is crucial; for example, a fitness YouTuber might benefit from writing a monthly column for a fitness magazine or website, resonating with their established audience. The key to success in column writing is consistency and quality. Regular, high-quality contributions are vital as columnists are often perceived as experts whose opinions can influence public perception.

Creators should leverage their columns to delve deeper into topics they cover in their videos, offering additional insights and value. This strategy enriches the content and reinforces the creator's expertise in their field.

To successfully implement column writing, creators should develop a unique voice that distinguishes them from other writers. Building relationships with editors through regular communication and reliability can lead to long-term collaborations, which are beneficial for sustained growth and visibility. Additionally, promoting the column through their YouTube channel and social media platforms can drive traffic to the publishing platform, increasing readership and enhancing the creator's influence.

Monetized

EVENTS, TRIPS, AND TOURS

Events, trips, and tours represent a sophisticated business model that leverages high-value activities and offers a dual advantage: they provide substantial revenue opportunities for creators and deliver unique, memorable experiences for their audience.

This model can transform passive viewers into active participants. The strong connection between creators and their audience, nurtured through consistent online interaction, lays the groundwork for successful event organization. The audience's familiarity with and trust in the creator increases the likelihood of participation in exclusive events, making it a viable business model.

Moreover, these events provide an opportunity to diversify revenue streams. Unlike ad-based or sponsorship income, which can fluctuate, events and tours offer a more stable and often higher income potential. The high-dollar value of these activities, especially when carefully tailored to match the audience's interests and willingness to pay, can significantly boost a creator's earnings.

For the audience, these events offer an unparalleled experience to engage with content they are passionate about in a real-world setting. The exclusivity of these events creates a sense of belonging and community among participants, deepening their connection to the creator and the content. This enhanced engagement benefits the audience and fosters loyalty, thereby contributing to the creator's long-term success and brand strength.

The model also allows for scalability. From local meetups and virtual tours, creators can gradually expand to more elaborate and extensive trips and retreats, scaling the business with their growing audience and resources.

Organizing exclusive events, trips, and tours is a strategic business model for content creators. It capitalizes on the existing audience base for financial gain. It strengthens the creator-audience

Monetized relationship, providing a unique, high-value experience that reinforces the creator's brand and fosters a loyal community.

Identify Key Themes

The success of themed tours hinges on their alignment with the channel's content. This alignment ensures the tours resonate with the audience's interests and preferences. For instance, a history-focused YouTube channel would naturally align with tours of historical landmarks, offering an enriching experience that extends the channel's educational content into real-world exploration.

Scout Locations

Thorough research and scouting of potential locations are crucial. This step ensures that the chosen locations are relevant to the tour's theme and logistically feasible and safe for attendees. The aim is to provide an immersive and seamless experience that mirrors the quality and focus of the channel's content.

Partnering with local guides or subject matter experts adds depth and authenticity to the tours. These collaborations can provide unique insights and perspectives, enhancing the overall educational value of the experience.

Randall Carlson's geologic feature tours exemplify this approach. His deep knowledge of geological and historical mysteries translates into tours that are not just journeys but educational experiences, allowing attendees to explore and understand these themes in real-world settings.

- **Planning**: Begin with smaller, local tours to gauge interest and refine logistics before scaling to more ambitious destinations.
- **Marketing**: Utilize the YouTube channel for promotion, leveraging teaser videos or testimonials to attract potential participants.

Monetized

- **Safety and Compliance**: Rigorously ensure that all tours comply with travel regulations and safety guidelines, prioritizing the safety and well-being of all participants.

Workshop Retreats

Workshop retreats blend education with leisure, targeting audiences eager to deepen their knowledge or skills in a relaxing environment. This model appeals to those who seek more than just passive content consumption, offering a hands-on learning experience in a serene setting. Living Web Farms does a great job of bringing people together to discuss niche topics.

- **Curate Content**: Tailor the workshop content to reflect the channel's niche, ensuring it appeals to the audience's known interests.
- **Select Venues**: Choose venues that facilitate the workshops and provide a relaxing and enjoyable environment.
- **Include Guest Speakers or Trainers**: Enrich the retreats with contributions from industry experts or influencers, adding diverse perspectives and expertise.

A fitness YouTuber promoting a wellness retreat is a practical illustration. Such a retreat could combine fitness sessions, nutritional workshops, and mindfulness activities, offering a holistic experience aligned with the channel's focus.

- **Scheduling**: Create a balanced itinerary interspersing educational sessions with leisure activities and sufficient free time.
- **Partnerships**: Form collaborations with relevant brands for equipment, materials, or sponsorships, enhancing the quality and reach of the retreat.

Collaborations with Travel Agencies

Partnering with travel agencies streamlines the organization of tours, providing professional logistical support. This collaboration allows

Monetized

content creators to focus on the content and experience aspect while leaving the intricate details of travel planning to experts.

- **Choose the Right Partner**: Select agencies with experience in the specific type of planned tours, ensuring they can meet the unique needs of your audience.
- **Customized Packages**: Work closely with the agency to develop tailor-made packages to reflect the channel's theme and cater to the audience's preferences.

Adventure travel vloggers creating custom adventure tours, like hiking or diving expeditions, in collaboration with travel agencies is a prime example of this strategy. These partnerships allow for the creation of unique and exciting experiences that are both safe and well-organized.

- **Negotiate Terms**: Establish clear terms regarding roles, responsibilities, and how revenue will be shared.
- **Quality Control**: Ensure that the quality and standards of the tours align with the brand and meet the audience's expectations, maintaining the creator's reputation and trust.

Monetized

ENTERTAINMENT, MEDIA, AND NEWS CHANNELS

Entertainment, Media, and News channels entertain, inform, and create immersive experiences that foster deep connections with audiences. The rise of digital media consumption has significantly shifted how viewers interact with entertainment and news content, making these channels particularly pivotal in the online ecosystem.

The global digital media market is witnessing exponential growth, driven by increasing internet penetration and the proliferation of smart devices. For Entertainment and Media channels, this surge is bolstered by the popularity of streaming services and user-generated content, which have transformed traditional entertainment paradigms. Meanwhile, News channels have found a new life online, reaching broader audiences who prefer real-time, accessible, and diverse news sources over conventional media outlets.

What sets Entertainment, Media, and News channels apart is their dynamic content, which ranges from movie reviews and celebrity interviews to real-time news coverage and satirical commentary. These genres demand constant innovation and adaptation to stay relevant and engaging. The audience for these channels is not just passive viewers but active participants, often seeking a more immersive and interactive experience.

The key to success for these channels lies in understanding and leveraging the nature of their audience's engagement. Viewers of Entertainment and Media channels often seek escapism, novelty, and community, while News channel viewers demand accuracy, diverse perspectives, and timely updates. This distinct audience engagement offers unique monetization opportunities, from super chat donations during live streams to crowdfunding initiatives for special projects and event coverage.

To thrive in this competitive space, creators must be adaptable and constantly innovating to meet the evolving demands of their audience. Whether it's through interactive live events, in-depth analysis, or behind-the-scenes content, these channels have the potential to create deeply engaging experiences that resonate with a wide range of viewers.

This chapter delves into specific monetization strategies tailored for Entertainment, Media, and News channels. We will explore how leveraging the unique aspects of these genres can lead to successful business models, ensuring sustainability and growth in the rapidly changing digital media landscape.

INTERACTIVE LIVE STREAMS / SUPER CHATS

Interactive live streaming involves broadcasting real-time video content to an audience over the internet, creating opportunities for direct interaction between the host and viewers. This dynamic form of content delivery has gained significant traction due to its immediacy and the ability to foster genuine connections with audiences. Unlike pre-recorded videos, live streams offer a sense of urgency and authenticity, making viewers feel more engaged and valued. This is crucial for content creators because it creates a more intimate and engaging experience, which can increase viewer retention, loyalty, and community building. Additionally, live streaming opens up various monetization opportunities, mainly through features like Super Chats and donations, which allow creators to generate income directly from their viewers during the broadcast.

Several platforms support live streaming, each with unique features and audience demographics. YouTube Live, integrated into the world's largest video-sharing platform, offers extensive reach and robust monetization options, including Super Chats and channel memberships. Twitch, primarily known for gaming content, has a highly interactive community and features such as Bits and subscriptions for monetization. Facebook Live leverages Facebook's massive user base to reach diverse audiences and offers Stars (a form of donation) and fan subscriptions. Instagram Live, popular among younger audiences, is ideal for casual and personal interactions, with monetization options including badges that viewers can purchase during live streams. Smaller platforms like Mixer (now defunct but historically significant) and DLive cater to niche communities and offer alternative monetization methods.

Monetized

Setup

Investing in the right equipment and software ensures a professional and smooth live-streaming experience. A high-quality webcam or DSLR camera is necessary for clear video, and a good-quality microphone ensures clear and crisp audio. Proper lighting setup enhances video quality and eliminates shadows, while a powerful computer is needed to handle streaming software and manage live interactions without lag. A stable, high-speed internet connection is critical to prevent buffering and ensure a seamless broadcast.

Setting up live streaming involves several technical steps. Streaming software like OBS Studio (Open Broadcaster Software) or Streamlabs OBS is essential for managing your live stream. These programs allow you to integrate various elements like overlays, alerts, and multiple camera angles. Platform integration involves linking your streaming software to your chosen platform (YouTube, Twitch, etc.) using stream keys and following the platform-specific setup guides. Conducting test streams is vital to ensure everything works correctly, including checking audio levels, video quality, and internet stability. A backup plan for technical issues, such as an alternative internet connection or secondary devices, is also advisable.

Engaging with your viewers

Engaging your audience during a live stream is crucial for maintaining their interest and encouraging interaction. Acknowledge new viewers, respond to comments, and mention regular participants by name to make them feel valued. Conducting polls or hosting Q&A sessions during the stream can also engage viewers. Including interactive elements like games, challenges, or live reactions to viewer suggestions can further enhance engagement.

Creating engaging content for live streams involves planning and outlining your stream's structure and leading topics to keep it organized and engaging. Maintaining authenticity in interactions is essential, as viewers appreciate genuine and relatable content.

Monetized

Overlays, transitions, and visual effects can enhance the viewing experience.

Monetizing through Super Chats and donations allows viewers to financially support creators during live streams, providing an income stream and encouraging higher viewer engagement. Super Chats allow viewers to pay to have their messages highlighted during a live stream, making them more visible to the host and audience. Donations are direct contributions from viewers through platforms like PayPal or integrated services within streaming platforms.

To maximize earnings, it's crucial to encourage viewer contributions by regularly reminding viewers of the donation and Super Chat options. Offering incentives, such as shoutouts, exclusive content, or participation in particular segments, can also encourage contributions. Providing exclusive access to behind-the-scenes content, private streams, or one-on-one interactions and offering merchandise or digital downloads as rewards for high-tier contributions can further incentivize viewer support. Highlighting and acknowledging donors through on-screen alerts and personal thank-yous during the stream or in follow-up communications is also essential.

Popular gaming streamers like Ninja or Pokimane have monetized their live streams through donations and Super Chats. In contrast, educational streamers who offer live tutorials or classes have effectively engaged their audience. Consistency, community building, and adaptability are critical lessons learned from top content creators. Regular streaming schedules help build a loyal audience, foster a sense of community, encourage viewer support and engagement, and continuously adapt content and monetization strategies based on audience feedback and trends, which can lead to success.

Setting clear guidelines for viewer behavior and interaction, utilizing moderation tools to manage inappropriate comments, and actively seeking and responding to audience feedback to improve the streaming experience is essential for managing audience expectations and moderation.

CROWDFUNDING

Crowdfunding has become a powerful tool for content creators to finance their projects and initiatives. By harnessing the collective financial power of a large audience, crowdfunding allows creators to raise the necessary funds without relying on traditional funding sources like loans or investors. This democratized approach to fundraising is particularly beneficial for creators seeking to maintain creative control and build a direct connection with their audience.

Crowdfunding involves soliciting small contributions from many people, typically via online platforms. These platforms give creators the tools to present their projects, engage with potential backers, and manage the fundraising process. Understanding the intricacies of crowdfunding is crucial for any content creator looking to leverage this method to support their endeavors.

Crowdfunding is a method of raising capital through the collective efforts of friends, family, fans, customers, and individual investors. This approach taps into the collective power of a large pool of individuals—primarily online via dedicated crowdfunding platforms—and leverages their networks for greater reach and exposure. Unlike traditional fundraising methods, crowdfunding allows content creators to showcase their projects to a global audience, enabling them to gain financial support and build a community of engaged followers.

Crowdfunding campaigns typically offer various incentives or rewards to backers in exchange for their financial contributions. These rewards can range from simple thank-you notes to exclusive content, merchandise, or early access to the final product. The key to a successful crowdfunding campaign lies in its ability to tell a compelling story, offer valuable rewards, and engage the audience throughout the campaign.

Several crowdfunding platforms have become synonymous with the industry, offering unique features and catering to different projects. Among the most popular are Kickstarter and GoFundMe.

Kickstarter is widely recognized for its focus on creative projects, including film, music, art, theater, games, comics, design, photography, and more. Kickstarter operates on an all-or-nothing funding model, meaning creators must reach their funding goal within a specified time frame to receive funds. This model encourages backers to promote the campaign, increasing the likelihood of achieving the funding goal.

GoFundMe, on the other hand, is known for its flexibility and ease of use, making it suitable for a wide range of projects, including personal causes, medical expenses, and community initiatives. Unlike Kickstarter, GoFundMe allows creators to keep the funds they raise even if they don't reach their initial goal, providing more flexibility in managing campaign finances.

Both platforms offer robust tools for campaign management, including analytics, communication tools, and integration with social media to help creators maximize their reach and engagement.

Planning a Crowdfunding Campaign

The foundation of a successful crowdfunding campaign is meticulous planning. Setting clear goals and objectives is paramount. These goals should be specific, measurable, achievable, relevant, and time-bound (SMART). Clear objectives provide direction and help track progress, ensuring the campaign remains focused and on track.

Identifying your target audience is another critical step. Understanding who will most likely support your project allows you to effectively tailor your messaging and marketing efforts. Conducting thorough market research to identify your potential backers' demographics, interests, and behaviors can significantly enhance the chances of a successful campaign. Engaging with your audience before launching the campaign can also build anticipation and establish a base of supporters ready to contribute from day one.

Crafting a Compelling Campaign

A compelling campaign narrative is essential for capturing the interest and support of potential backers. Your campaign story should be engaging and authentic and convey the purpose and impact of your project. Highlight the problem you are solving or the unique value your project brings. Personal stories and emotional appeals can be particularly effective in connecting with your audience.

Creating high-quality visual and video content is equally important. Videos, in particular, are powerful tools for conveying your message and demonstrating your passion for the project. A well-produced campaign video can make a significant difference in attracting backers. Ensure that your visuals are professional, clear, and visually appealing, as this reflects the quality and seriousness of your project.

Offering Rewards and Incentives

Designing attractive reward tiers is a strategic component of any crowdfunding campaign. Rewards should be enticing and appropriately valued to motivate backers at various contribution levels. A range of rewards, from small tokens of appreciation for minimal contributions to exclusive experiences or products for higher-tier backers, can cater to a broader audience.

Ensuring reward fulfillment is crucial for maintaining trust and credibility. Communicate the timeline for reward delivery and keep your promises. Delays and unmet expectations can damage your reputation and hinder future campaigns. Transparency and regular updates about the status of rewards can help manage backer expectations and maintain their support.

Monetized

Promoting Your Crowdfunding Campaign

Effective promotion is key to a successful crowdfunding campaign. Leveraging social media and your existing audience can create a strong foundation of support. Regular updates, engaging content, and calls to action can drive traffic to your campaign page and encourage contributions.

Partnering with influencers and other channels can expand your reach beyond your immediate network. Influencers who align with your project's values and goals can provide valuable endorsements and attract new backers. Collaborations and cross-promotions with other content creators can also enhance visibility and credibility.

Managing the Campaign

Active management of your crowdfunding campaign is essential for maintaining momentum. Monitoring progress and engagement allows you to adjust your strategies as needed. Responding promptly to backer inquiries and feedback demonstrates your commitment and fosters a sense of community.

Updating backers regularly about the progress of the campaign and the project builds trust and keeps them engaged. Transparency about challenges or changes is crucial for maintaining backer confidence and support.

Post-Campaign Actions

Once your campaign concludes, fulfilling rewards and delivering on promises is your priority. Ensuring timely and accurate reward fulfillment is critical for maintaining your reputation and fostering long-term relationships with backers.

Maintaining relationships with your backers for future campaigns can provide a loyal base of supporters. Regular updates on the project's progress, sharing successes, and acknowledging their contributions can turn backers into long-term fans and advocates for your work.

Monetized

Case Studies and Success Stories

Examining successful crowdfunding campaigns in your niche can provide valuable insights and inspiration. For example, the Exploding Kittens card game campaign on Kickstarter became a massive success, exceeding its funding goal by millions. Key takeaways from successful campaigns often include the importance of a compelling narrative, high-quality visuals, effective use of social media, and strong community engagement.

Common Pitfalls and How to Avoid Them

Despite the potential for success, crowdfunding campaigns can face several common pitfalls. Failing to set realistic funding goals, poor planning, and ineffective communication can derail a campaign. Learning from failed campaigns is as essential as studying successful ones. Identifying potential risks, such as production delays or budget overruns, and developing mitigation strategies can help avoid these pitfalls and increase the likelihood of a successful campaign.

EVENT COVERAGE CONTRACTS

Event coverage represents a significant opportunity for content creators to expand their influence and generate revenue. As the digital landscape evolves, the demand for high-quality event content has surged, with audiences eager to experience events vicariously through their favorite creators. The role of content creators in event coverage is multifaceted, encompassing the capture of critical moments, behind-the-scenes footage, and exclusive interviews. This dynamic role allows creators to offer unique perspectives that traditional media outlets may not provide, thereby adding value to the event and enriching the audience's experience.

Events suitable for coverage by content creators are diverse and include industry conferences, product launches, music festivals, sporting events, and cultural gatherings. Each type of event offers different opportunities and challenges, requiring a tailored approach to maximize impact. Whether it's a tech expo or a music concert, the essence of successful event coverage lies in understanding the event's core message and the audience's interests.

Negotiating Event Coverage Contracts

Negotiating event coverage contracts is crucial in securing work and ensuring that both the creator and the event organizers have clear, aligned expectations. Approaching event organizers requires a professional and strategic method. Start by researching the event and identifying key decision-makers. Craft a compelling proposal highlighting your unique value proposition—what you can offer that sets you apart from other content creators.

When setting expectations and deliverables, clarity is paramount. Define the scope of work, including the type of content to be produced, the timeline for delivery, and any specific requirements from the event organizers. This can encompass live streaming sessions, pre-recorded videos, social media posts, or a combination thereof. Ensure that all terms, including payment, usage rights, and exclusivity clauses, are clearly articulated in the contract to avoid misunderstandings.

Preparing for Event Coverage

Thorough preparation is essential to deliver high-quality event coverage. Gathering the necessary equipment and gear tailored to the event's needs. This might include cameras, microphones, lighting equipment, and backup storage devices. Ensuring that you have the right tools can significantly impact the quality of your content.

Planning your content strategy involves understanding the event's schedule and identifying key moments that resonate with your audience. Create a content calendar outlining what you will capture and when, allowing flexibility to adapt to unexpected opportunities. Engaging with your audience before the event through polls or Q&A sessions can also provide valuable insights into what they are most interested in seeing.

Capturing High-Quality Content

When capturing high-quality content, attention to detail and technical proficiency are vital. Ensure your equipment is set up correctly and tested beforehand for recording and live-streaming events. This includes checking sound levels, lighting conditions, and internet connectivity for live streams. Position yourself strategically to capture the best angles and moments, and be prepared to move quickly to follow the action.

Interviewing event participants and guests adds depth to your coverage. Prepare thoughtful questions that align with the event's themes and your audience's interests. Ensure that interviews are well-lit and that audio is clear. Building rapport with interviewees beforehand can help them feel more comfortable and provide candid responses.

Monetized

Monetizing Event Coverage

Monetizing event coverage involves several strategies. Charging coverage fees is a direct approach, where you negotiate a fee for your services with the event organizers. This fee should reflect the scope of work, the expected quality of content, and the value you bring to the event.

Creating sponsored content and partnerships offers another revenue stream. Collaborate with brands that align with the event's theme and your audience's interests. Sponsored content can range from branded segments within your coverage to dedicated posts or shout-outs. Ensure all sponsorship agreements are transparent and the content remains authentic to maintain audience trust.

Promoting Event Coverage

Promotion is vital to maximizing the reach and impact of your event coverage. Utilize social media platforms for cross-promotion, sharing teasers, behind-the-scenes snippets, and live updates to build anticipation. Engaging with event attendees and your audience through comments, live chats, and interactive posts can enhance the coverage's reach and engagement.

Leveraging hashtags, tagging the event's official accounts, and collaborating with other influencers or creators attending the event can further amplify your content's visibility. Post-event, continue to engage your audience by sharing highlight reels, bloopers, or extended interviews.

Post-Event Actions

After the event, the work continues. Editing and publishing high-quality content promptly keeps the momentum and maintains audience interest. Focus on creating polished, engaging videos highlighting the event's key moments and insights.

Providing detailed reports and feedback to event organizers is also crucial. This demonstrates your professionalism and can lead to

Monetized

repeat business and referrals. Include metrics such as viewer engagement, reach, and any feedback from your audience to show the impact of your coverage.

Monetized

GAMING CONTENT CREATORS AND STREAMERS

As gaming continues to dominate as a leading form of entertainment, these creators provide engaging content and cultivate vibrant communities around their passion for gaming. The rapid expansion of the gaming industry has reshaped how audiences interact with digital content, making gaming channels a cornerstone of the online ecosystem.

The global gaming market is experiencing unprecedented growth, driven by technological advancements, increasing internet accessibility, and the proliferation of gaming platforms. For gaming content creators, this surge is propelled by diverse areas such as game development, game mod content, and hosting tournaments and servers. These facets have revolutionized the traditional gaming experience, offering endless opportunities for innovation and engagement.

What distinguishes gaming content creators and streamers is their ability to produce a wide range of content, from in-depth game development tutorials to captivating live streams of competitive tournaments. The gaming community is not just a passive audience; it is an active and engaged network of enthusiasts who seek interaction, entertainment, and a sense of belonging.

The key to success for gaming content creators lies in understanding and harnessing the unique dynamics of their audience's engagement. Gamers often look for immersive experiences, expert insights, and community-driven content. This distinct audience engagement presents unique monetization opportunities, from supporting game

Monetized

development projects through crowdfunding to generating revenue from hosting and participating in tournaments and server management.

To excel in this competitive and ever-changing landscape, gaming content creators must be versatile and innovative, continuously adapting to meet the evolving needs of their audience. Whether through detailed game development guides, exciting mod showcases, or organizing and streaming high-stakes tournaments, these creators have the potential to craft deeply engaging content that resonates with gamers worldwide.

This chapter explores specific monetization strategies tailored for gaming content creators and streamers. We will explore how leveraging the unique aspects of game development, game mod content, and hosting tournaments and servers can lead to successful and sustainable business models in the rapidly expanding gaming industry.

GAME DEVELOPMENT

In the rapidly evolving digital media landscape, content creators constantly seek innovative ways to diversify their revenue streams and deepen audience engagement. The intersection of YouTube content creation and game development presents a compelling business model, especially in Mobile, Virtual Reality (VR), and Augmented Reality (AR) gaming. This synergy capitalizes on the unique strengths of both platforms – the broad reach and established viewer base of YouTube channels and the immersive, interactive nature of modern gaming.

The justification for this business model lies in the inherent alignment of audience interests and content themes. YouTube content creators often cultivate a dedicated following based on specific genres or topics. By developing games that resonate with these themes, creators can tap into a ready-made audience eager to engage with content in new, interactive ways. This approach enhances user experience and ensures a higher likelihood of game adoption and success.

Furthermore, the VR/AR gaming sector, though growing, is still relatively nascent, offering content creators an opportunity to enter a market with less saturation compared to traditional gaming platforms. This presents a unique advantage of higher visibility and potentially quicker market penetration for new entrants. By leveraging the storytelling and audience-building skills honed through YouTube content creation, these creators can introduce innovative gaming experiences that stand out in the market.

The audience, already engaged with the content creator's brand, becomes a natural advocate for the game, facilitating organic marketing and promotion. This audience can also provide invaluable feedback during development, ensuring that the game meets user expectations and preferences. In essence, the creator's YouTube

Monetized

channel serves as a direct line to potential users, significantly reducing marketing costs and increasing the efficacy of promotional efforts.

Steam is a colossal global marketplace, a hub for gamers and developers alike. Its vast user base and diverse catalog make it an ideal platform for launching new games, especially in the VR/AR domain. The relatively lower level of competition in the VR/AR space compared to traditional gaming platforms presents a unique opportunity for content creators. New entrants can quickly capture significant market share by offering innovative experiences that stand out in this less crowded market.

Recent advances in platforms like Unreal Engine, Godot, or GameMaker Studio allow content creators to develop games cost-effectively. These platforms are accessible and scalable, making them ideal for YouTubers new to game development. They will also bring the cost of creating a game down to accessible levels for small businesses. Tutorials or behind-the-scenes content on game development can further engage the channel's audience.

Channel-Themed Games

Games that align with the themes and content of a YouTube channel have the advantage of an established audience base. These games resonate with the viewers' interests, making them more appealing to followers of the channel. Fans naturally engage with games showcasing their interests on the channel. This familiarity breeds a sense of connection and loyalty, encouraging them to support the game. The design process should involve integrating elements, characters, or popular themes on the channel. Engaging with the audience to gather feedback during development ensures that the game aligns with their expectations and enhances their connection to the channel's content.

User Engagement

Interactive games serve as a powerful platform for deepening audience engagement. These games offer an immersive and interactive experience critical to retaining viewer interest and loyalty. Engaged users are likelier to remain loyal and promote the game through word-of-mouth. This consistent engagement is essential for sustaining a steady revenue stream and expanding the game's reach. Features such as multiplayer modes, community challenges, and integration with social media platforms should be incorporated to maximize user engagement. These elements encourage active participation and foster a sense of community among players.

Revenue Through In-App Purchases

In-app purchases present a direct and effective monetization strategy for games. They provide a way for players to enhance their gaming experience while contributing to the game's revenue. This model allows for continuous revenue generation beyond the initial sale of the game. It's a sustainable approach to monetization, balancing ongoing income with player satisfaction. Developing a well-balanced in-app purchase strategy involves creating purchasable items or features that add value to the game without disrupting the gameplay or creating a pay-to-win scenario.

Cross-Promotion Opportunities

The symbiotic relationship between a YouTube channel and its game offers immense cross-promotion opportunities. Each platform can be used to amplify the other's presence and reach. This cross-promotion enhances the visibility of the game and the channel, creating a mutually beneficial relationship. It opens up new avenues for audience growth and engagement. Utilizing the YouTube channel to showcase game development progress, updates, and special features is effective. Including references or easter eggs in the game that link back to the channel strengthens this connection.

Real-World Examples and Case Studies

PewDiePie's Tuber Simulator and **Beat Saber** serve as excellent examples. Tuber Simulator mirrors PewDiePie's content, drawing in his vast audience, while Beat Saber's VR rhythm gameplay has

Monetized

captivated a broad audience, offering exposure opportunities for growing musicians.

A robust marketing strategy, including teasers, trailers, and playthroughs, coupled with collaborations for cross-promotion, can significantly amplify the game's reach. Involving the community in the development process through beta testing and feedback sessions improves the game and fosters viewer loyalty and investment in the game's success.

GAME MOD DEVELOPMENT

Game mod development presents an advantageous business model for YouTube content creators, particularly in entertainment and media. This strategy capitalizes on the unique intersection between content creation, audience engagement, and the expansive world of gaming.

A primary appeal of game mod development lies in its cost-effectiveness and efficiency. Creating a mod is significantly less resource-intensive than the daunting task of developing a full-fledged game. It requires fewer financial investments and less development time, making it an accessible venture for content creators who may not have extensive programming skills or large budgets. This accessibility allows creators to experiment with game development without the substantial risks of creating a complete game from scratch.

Furthermore, game mods tap into pre-existing audiences of popular games. This existing user base is a critical asset, as it provides a ready-made audience eager to explore new content within their favorite games. By developing mods that resonate with these established communities, content creators can effectively piggyback on the game's popularity, ensuring a higher visibility and engagement rate than starting an audience from ground zero.

The symbiotic relationship between a game mod and its parent game also offers a unique marketing advantage. Fans of the game are often enthusiastic about exploring mods that add new dimensions or features to their gaming experience. This enthusiasm translates into a more engaged audience for the content creator, who can leverage this interest to enhance their brand visibility and deepen viewer loyalty.

In essence, game mod development is a strategic entry point for YouTube content creators into the gaming industry. It allows them to

Monetized

leverage their existing content creation and audience engagement skills while exploring new creative territories with lower risks and higher potential returns.

Leveraging Existing Popularity

The strategy of leveraging the existing popularity of games like Minecraft and Fortnite is an intelligent move for content creators looking to expand their reach. These games come with vast, active communities continually seeking new experiences within the game. By introducing mods that align with a YouTube channel's brand or theme, creators can tap into this ready audience. The implementation involves crafting mods such as character skins or unique in-game items that echo the channel's ethos. Whether these are imbued with humor, style, or specific thematic elements, the goal is to make them compelling enough to capture the gamers' attention. This approach enhances the gaming experience and serves as a subtle yet effective marketing tool for the content creator.

Sell a Character

Selling custom mods, particularly in games like Minecraft and Fortnite, opens a direct revenue stream for content creators—platforms such as the Minecraft Marketplace or Unreal Marketplace present ideal venues for this endeavor. The key to success here is in designing mods that are both distinctive and high quality. These creations should genuinely reflect the channel's brand, ensuring they stand out in the marketplace. When listing these mods, clear communication about their origin and story can significantly enhance brand recognition among the gaming community.

Community Building

Mods have the unique ability to foster sub-communities within the broader audience of a game. By creating a mod that resonates with players, a content creator can cultivate loyalty and boost viewership for their channel. Effective community building involves engaging with players through forums, social media, and in-game interactions. Organizing events or competitions centered around the mod can further solidify this community, creating a dedicated fan base beyond the game itself.

Creative Freedom

The realm of game mods offers an expansive canvas for creativity. Content creators can experiment with various aspects of modding, ranging from aesthetic designs to gameplay mechanics. The objective is to ensure that these mods align with the channel's brand and appeal to the target audience's preferences and interests. This creative freedom allows content creators to express their unique style and vision within the game, adding a personal touch that resonates with players.

Collaborations with Game Developers

Collaborating with original game developers can open doors to more sophisticated mod development and mutual promotion. This approach involves reaching out to developers for potential partnerships, from co-developing a mod to officially featuring it in the game. Such collaborations can enhance the credibility of the moderator and, by extension, the YouTube channel, leading to increased visibility and growth.

Examples like custom Minecraft character skins developed by YouTubers and unique Fortnite characters that have gained popularity illustrate the potential of mod development. Some of these creations have even caught the attention of game developers like Epic Games, leading to official adoption. Additionally, listing mods in marketplaces like Unreal Marketplace has proven beneficial for creators, though it comes with the risk of losing control over how the brand is used.

Successful mod development requires thoroughly understanding the game's modding tools and guidelines. This research and development phase is crucial to creating a mod that aligns seamlessly with the game's mechanics and the channel's brand. Once developed, strategic marketing and promotion are critical. Utilizing the YouTube channel, social media, and other platforms to showcase the mod's features is

Monetized

essential. Keeping the mod relevant involves regular community interaction, feedback collection, and updates. Networking and collaboration with game developers and modders can provide valuable insights and opportunities. Lastly, a well-thought-out monetization and sales strategy tailored to the target audience and the mod's value is critical for financial success.

GAME TOURNAMENTS

Online gaming tournaments present a lucrative business model for gaming, entertainment, and media content creators. This model capitalizes on the burgeoning esports industry, which has recently witnessed rapid growth and mainstream acceptance. The appeal of these tournaments lies in their ability to draw large, dedicated audiences, comprising both players and spectators, who are deeply invested in the gaming world.

For content creators, organizing and hosting gaming tournaments offers multiple benefits. Firstly, it aligns perfectly with their existing content and audience interests, ensuring high engagement. This alignment makes it a natural extension of their channel rather than an unrelated venture, increasing the likelihood of success. Additionally, these tournaments create unique content opportunities, enabling creators to diversify their offerings and keep their audience engaged with fresh, dynamic content.

The gaming content's audience is significant in numbers and engagement. Fans of gaming channels are often passionate, loyal, and actively involved in the gaming community. This high level of engagement makes them more likely to participate in or watch tournaments, contributing to higher viewer numbers and longer watch times. Moreover, the competitive nature of these tournaments adds an element of excitement and spectacle, further enhancing viewer engagement.

The interactive nature of online gaming tournaments also opens up avenues for audience participation, an essential aspect of community building. Content creators can strengthen their relationship with their audience by involving viewers in the tournament, either as participants or through interactive features like live chats and polls. This enhanced engagement not only boosts the immediate success of the game but also fosters long-term loyalty to the channel.

Monetized

From a business standpoint, these tournaments offer a diverse revenue stream. Sponsorships, advertising, and participant fees contribute to the revenue while providing opportunities for brand partnerships and collaborations. Moreover, the content generated from these tournaments - including live streams, highlights, and player interviews - can be monetized and used to attract new subscribers.

In summary, the business model of hosting online gaming tournaments aligns seamlessly with the goals and audience of entertainment and media content creators. It leverages the passionate and engaged gaming community for success while offering a multifaceted content creation and monetization approach.

Organizing and Hosting

The success of an online gaming tournament hinges on meticulous planning and execution. The first crucial step is identifying the target audience. This decision shapes the entire event, from the selection of games to the tournament format and promotional activities. A tournament aimed at casual gamers might focus on fun, community-oriented games and a relaxed format. In contrast, one targeting competitive players would opt for games with a competitive edge and a more structured format.

Selecting a suitable game is pivotal. The chosen game should resonate with the channel's existing audience and have a solid and active community. Popular games with dedicated followings ensure higher participation and viewer engagement. Moreover, the game's suitability for competitive play and spectator appeal are essential factors.

The tournament format is another consideration. It should be engaging, easy to understand for viewers, and compatible with the selected game. Standard formats include knockout, league, or round-robin, each offering different advantages in terms of viewer engagement and tournament duration.

Monetized

Logistics form the backbone of the event. This involves detailed planning of the registration process, schedule, rules, and the choice of platform for hosting the tournament. Ensuring a seamless and user-friendly experience for both participants and viewers is essential.

Sponsorship Opportunities

Securing sponsorships is a vital aspect of organizing a gaming tournament. The first step is to identify potential sponsors whose brands align with the gaming community. This could include gaming hardware companies, software developers, or lifestyle brands that appeal to the gaming demographic.

Developing a range of sponsorship packages can attract a variety of sponsors. These packages can offer different visibility and engagement opportunities, ranging from title sponsorships to in-game advertising and product placements.

An attractive prize pool is essential to draw participants and create excitement around the event. This can be achieved through sponsor donations or allocating a portion of the revenue generated from the event. The prize pool is a significant draw for participants and can be leveraged to market the tournament.

Live Streaming the Event

Choosing the right streaming platform is critical for reaching the desired audience. Factors such as audience reach, monetization options, and streaming quality play a significant role in this choice. Popular platforms like Twitch, YouTube, or Facebook Gaming offer different advantages depending on the target audience.

Content creation during the tournament extends beyond the live gameplay. It includes producing content such as game highlights, player interviews, and behind-the-scenes footage. This content enriches the viewer experience and provides additional material for post-event marketing.

Monetized

Monetizing the live stream is integral to the event's financial success. Methods like running ads, encouraging super chats, offering channel memberships, and providing exclusive content for subscribers can generate significant revenue.

Community Engagement

Engaging the audience is crucial for the success of the tournament. Interactive elements like live chats, audience polls, and predictions can significantly enhance viewer engagement. These features encourage viewers to actively participate in the event, creating a more immersive experience.

Social media promotion is essential for creating buzz around the tournament. Regular updates, teasers, and interactive posts on platforms like Twitter, Instagram, and Facebook help engage with the community and build anticipation for the event.

Post-tournament, creating follow-up content that recaps the event, highlights the best moments, and acknowledges participants and winners help maintain engagement. This content serves as a tool for audience retention and as promotional material for future events.

Marketing and Promotion

Developing a comprehensive marketing plan is essential. This should encompass social media campaigns, influencer partnerships, and engaging content teasers. A well-rounded marketing strategy ensures maximum reach and engagement.

Engaging with the community through forums, social media groups, and gaming platforms generates interest and buzz around the event. It also helps in understanding the audience's preferences and expectations.

Hosting pre-tournament events like Q&A sessions with participants, gaming workshops, or prediction contests builds excitement and anticipation for the main event. These activities also provide additional content opportunities and audience engagement touchpoints.

Post-Event Activities

Analyzing the tournament's success through metrics like viewer count, engagement rates, and participant feedback is crucial for continuous improvement. These insights help us understand what worked well and what can be improved in future tournaments.

Ongoing engagement with the community post-event can sustain interest in the channel and its future activities. This could involve regular updates, teasers for upcoming events, or interactive content that keeps the audience engaged.

By implementing these strategies, content creators can successfully organize and monetize online gaming tournaments, strengthen their community, enhance their brand, and create a loyal viewer base.

HOSTING A GAMING SERVER

Gaming has transcended from a pastime to a dynamic community-building and engagement platform. Hosting a gaming server is one of the most effective ways for content creators to foster a strong, interactive community. This strategy enhances the relationship between the creator and their audience and opens robust monetization avenues, mainly through subscription models.

Creating a Hub for Community Interaction

Hosting a gaming server allows content creators to create a centralized hub where their audience can congregate, interact, and collaborate. Unlike traditional social media platforms, where interactions are often superficial and fleeting, a dedicated gaming server offers a persistent and immersive environment. Players can engage in shared activities, participate in events, and form lasting connections with like-minded individuals.

A well-maintained server can become a vibrant community where players feel a sense of belonging. This environment fosters deeper engagement as players consume content passively and actively participate in the creator's ecosystem. The interactions on the server are not limited to gaming alone; they can extend to discussions about strategies, sharing fan art, or even organizing community-driven events.

Enhancing Creator-Audience Interaction

A gaming server provides a unique platform for content creators to interact directly with their audience. This direct engagement is invaluable as it humanizes the creator and strengthens the bond with the community. Creators can host live events, such as Q&A sessions, gameplay streams, or special in-game activities, where they can interact with their audience in real-time.

These interactions are more personal and impactful compared to other forms of communication. For instance, a creator hosting a live gaming session on their server can respond to questions, provide tips, and share insights on the spot. This immediacy and accessibility enhance the viewer's experience and foster a loyal community.

Monetization Through Subscription Models

Monetizing a gaming server can be effectively achieved through a subscription model. By offering exclusive server access as part of a subscription package, content creators can provide added value to their audience while generating a steady revenue stream. Here are several ways this can be implemented:

Exclusive Access: Subscribers can be given exclusive access to the server, creating a sense of exclusivity and privilege. This can include early access to new content, special in-game items, or reserved slots during peak times.

Premium Features: Creators can offer premium features or services to subscribers, such as custom game modes, unique skins, or enhanced support. These features enhance the gaming experience and provide tangible benefits to subscribers.

Community Events: Regularly scheduled events, such as tournaments, build contests, or themed game nights, can be exclusive to subscribers. These events not only provide entertainment but also promote community engagement and loyalty.

Direct Support: By subscribing, players can support their favorite creators directly. Many fans are willing to pay for the opportunity to contribute to the sustainability and growth of the community they cherish.

Monetized

Practical Considerations for Hosting a Server

To successfully implement a subscription-based gaming server, content creators must consider several practical aspects:

Server Stability: Ensure the server is stable and can handle the anticipated traffic. Downtime or lag can negatively impact the user experience.

Moderation: A dedicated team of moderators can help maintain a positive and respectful environment. Clear rules and active enforcement are essential to foster a welcoming community.

Content Updates: Regular and new content is crucial to keep the community engaged. This could include new game modes, seasonal events, or unique challenges.

Feedback Mechanism: Providing a channel for feedback allows subscribers to voice their opinions and suggestions. This can help tailor the server experience to better meet the community's needs.

Monetized

Monetized

Dear Reader,

As we reach the end of "Monetized," I want to extend my heartfelt thanks to you, the reader, for embarking on this journey with me. This book was crafted to provide the tools, insights, and strategies necessary to transform your passion into a profitable venture. Whether you are a content creator just starting or an experienced entrepreneur looking to diversify your income streams, I hope you have found the information presented here both valuable and inspiring.

The world of content creation is vast and ever-evolving. The strategies discussed in this book are designed to be adaptable and flexible, allowing you to find the right fit for your unique brand and audience. There are countless ways to monetize your content and build a sustainable income, from advertising revenue and affiliate marketing to merchandise sales and digital products.

As you progress, I encourage you to experiment with several strategies that resonate most with you. Test and refine them and see how they can be integrated into your business model. Remember, success in monetization often comes from persistence, creativity, and a willingness to adapt and learn.

Building a profitable content creation business is a journey of challenges and opportunities. It requires dedication, hard work, and a continuous drive to innovate. But with the right strategies and a clear understanding of your goals, you can achieve financial independence and turn your passion into a thriving enterprise.

I wish you the best of luck in your endeavors. May you succeed in the strategies you implement and continue to grow and prosper as a content creator and entrepreneur. Thank you for letting me be a part of your journey, and I look forward to seeing the incredible things you will achieve.

Happy monetizing!

ABOUT THE AUTHOR

Michael Piepkorn is a seasoned small business consultant and sourcing professional with over a decade of experience in the private and corporate sectors. Throughout his career, Michael has dedicated himself to helping franchisees and small businesses enhance sales, streamline operations, and achieve greater competitiveness in the marketplace. His expertise spans various business functions, including sales strategy, operational efficiency, and business development.

Michael's passion lies in empowering small businesses and supporting the cottage economy. He believes in the power of niche markets and local crafts to create a diverse and resilient economic landscape. His consulting work has helped numerous entrepreneurs and small business owners realize their full potential and thrive in competitive environments.

As an advocate for content creators, Michael's first book, "Monetized," offers invaluable insights and strategies to help creators turn their passion into profit. Drawing on his extensive experience and deep understanding of practical business principles, Michael provides grounded advice and actionable tips for monetizing content across various platforms.

Michael is based in the Midwest and is committed to fostering a community of innovative, prosperous, and resilient entrepreneurs. Through his work, he continues to inspire and guide others on their journey to financial independence and business success.

www.ingramcontent.com/pod-product-compliance
Lightning Source LLC
Chambersburg PA
CBHW050100230526
45470CB00004B/1606